Soaring
in the
Heaven
of
God's Love

Soaring
in the
Heaven
of
God's Love

An Exploration
into the Transformative
Power of the Bahá'í
Long Obligatory Prayer

Ted Brownstein

New Lands Press, Chicago, Illinois

The wisdom of obligatory prayer is this: That it caus-
eth a connection between the servant and the True One . . .

For a lover, there is no greater pleasure than to con-
verse with his beloved . . .

It is the greatest longing of every soul who is attracted
to the Kingdom of God to find time to turn with entire
devotion to his Beloved, so as to seek His bounty and
blessing and immerse himself in the ocean of communion,
entreaty and supplication.

—'Abdu'l-Bahá

. . . the long Obligatory Prayer should be
said at those times when one feeleth himself in a prayerful
mood. In truth, it hath been revealed in such wise that if it
be recited to a rock, that rock would stir and speak forth;
and if it be recited to a mountain, that mountain would
move and flow.

—Bahá'u'lláh

Contents

Foreword

Prayer is an expression of our deepest emotions. It creates a path to connection with the great subliminal mystery that both whispers within our souls and radiates throughout the cosmos. Encompassing a wide variety of forms, including poetry, music, chanting, recitation and spontaneous expression, prayer is a prime practice in all the world's religions.

This commentary draws on the sacred books of many traditional faiths, seeking to show facets of humanity's shared spiritual heritage. Even groups, such as Tibetan Buddhists, who consider themselves to be atheists and deny the existence of "god" share much in common with theistic faiths. Central features of their practice include sacred chanting and meditation that aim to tap into a transcendent spiritual reality. Each religious community has its unique language and expression. However, close examination will reveal that often apparent differences dissolve once the veil of names is stripped away.

Even secular humanists, who likewise deny the existence of "God," hold to beliefs in the sacredness of life and moral values greater than the needs and wants of individuals. The longing to reach beyond ourselves and draw inspiration from a greater reality is universal.

Among Bahá'í prayers, there are abundant reasons the Bahá'í Long Obligatory Prayer has special potency. I know of no other prayer that Bahá'u'lláh says has the power to animate rocks and mountains (understood figuratively as giving spiritual life to individuals and faith-based institutions). Its length alone allows the supplicant sufficient time to dismiss other concerns and become fully engaged in the prayer. The frequent change of body postures, serves the same end, to entirely engross the supplicant in communion with God. Meditating on the words of the prayer helps uplift one's thoughts. Awareness of its word choice and references to word pictures found in the world's sacred literature serve to connect one's mental thoughts to a rich tradition of wisdom.

This prayer serves to strengthen the ties between the reciter and her or his creator. Through the use of tangible metaphor and thought provoking statements of sacred principle, we are given a glimpse of God's Beauty and the supreme joy of nearness to His Presence. Central teachings of Bahá'u'lláh are expounded, either explicitly or implicitly in, dramatic, soul-stirring fashion. Found in the prayer are lessons in humankind's utter dependence on God's grace, the unity of all religions, independent investigation of truth, forgiveness, self-sacrifice and God's purpose to use progressive revelation to bring forth an ever-advancing civilization.

Continued learning on the depth and breadth of this prayer may serve to keep each day's recitation fresh and heartfelt.

> May your souls be illumined by the light of the Words of God, and may you become repositories of the mysteries of God, for no comfort is greater and no happiness is sweeter than spiritual comprehension of the divine teachings. If a man understands the real meaning of a poet's verses such as those of Shakespeare, he is pleased and rejoiced. How much greater his joy and pleasure when he perceives the reality of the Holy Scriptures and becomes informed of the mysteries of the Kingdom!
>
> —'ABDU'L-BAHÁ, *The Promulgation of Universal Peace*, 459

It is the author's hope that this brief and partial commentary will be an aid to that end and the continuation of a lifelong process.

May the study of this precious prayer bring you joy and boundless spiritual blessings.

The comments offered here are based solely on the English translation. Elucidating the subtle and more technical meanings hidden in the original Arabic is something I welcome, but leave to scholars knowledgeable in Arabic. All the comments expressed in this work are strictly opinions of the author and not an attempt to speak authoritatively. Whether you use this book for group study or private meditation, I hope it will aid you in your exploration of the prayer's beautiful and rich meaning.

Citation Notes

Quotations from the Bahá'í Writings are identified by author, book and page number or where the author's name is included in the title, by title and page number alone, such as *Proclamation of Bahá'u'lláh*, 118. Quotations from other sacred scriptures are identified by book and customary reference in each religious tradition, and religion, such as John 3:16. Christian Scripture, or Garland Sutra 11, Buddhist Scripture. The terms Hebrew Scripture and Christian Old Testament are used interchangeably, as they both refer to the body of sacred literature originally written in Hebrew/Aramaic as contained in the Jewish Bible. Quotes from secondary sources follow the same format but they are labelled to distinguish them from sacred scripture, such as *Mathnavi of Rumi*, Vol 1, Story VIII, Islámic poet.

When emphasizing a specific word or phrase in a citation, the key word or words are often shown in ***bold underline***. Such formatting is not original to the sacred text, but added at the author's discretion to aid in understanding the commentary and the relevance of the citation to the specific phrase in the Long Obligatory Prayer under discussion.

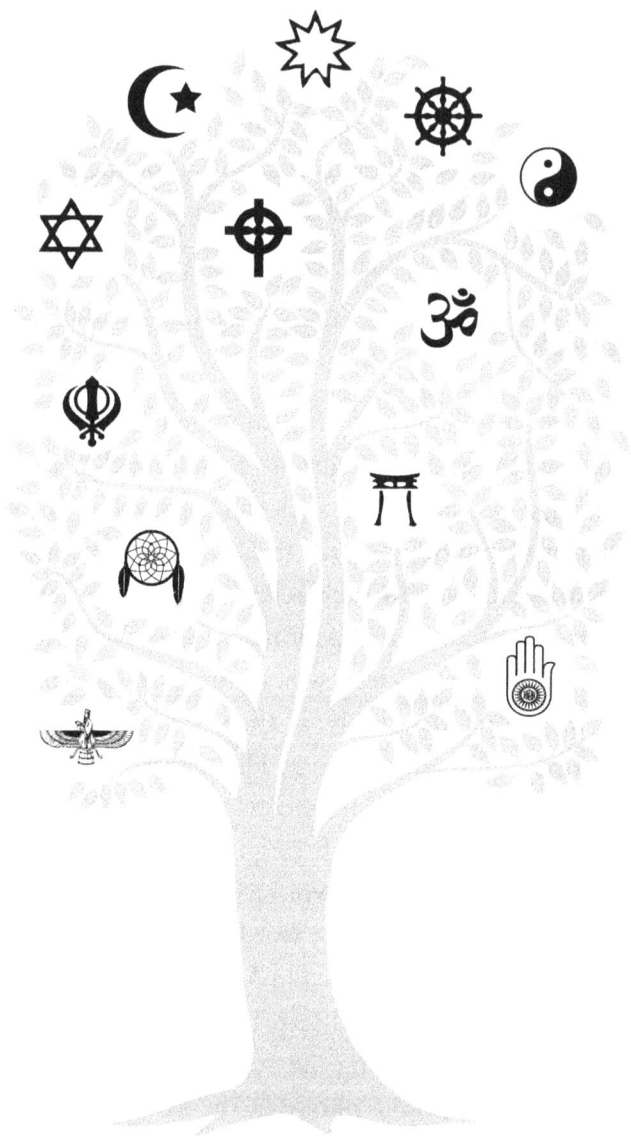

Prayer as a Pillar of Faith in All Religions

For the Great Spirit is everywhere; he hears the prayer of our minds and hearts, and it is not necessary to speak to him in a loud voice.

—BLACK ELK (as told to Joseph Epes Brown, *The Sacred Pipe*, 58, Native American Sioux tradition)

And I celebrate . . . the good and pious prayer for blessings, the benediction of the pious . . .

—ZEND-AVESTA (Visperad 1:7, Zoroastrian scripture)

Would that man could pray all day.

—JERUSALEM TALMUD (BERAKOT, 1.1, Jewish tradition)

When practicing contemplation, they should wish that all beings see truth as it is and be forever free of opposition and contention.

—FLOWER GARLAND SUTRA (or Avatamsaka Sutra 11, Buddhist scripture)

Pray incessantly.

—St Paul's *1st letter to the Thessalonians*
(1 Thessalonians 5:17, Christian scripture)

Establish regular prayer at the two ends of the day and at
the approaches of the night . . . This is the word of remembrance to those who remember.

—Qur'án (Surah 11:114,
Islámic scripture)

There is a polish for everything that becomes rusty, and the
polish for the heart is remembrance of God.

—Hadith (Bukhari 4,
Islámic tradition)

. . . in all Dispensations the law of prayer hath constituted
a fundamental element of the Revelation of all the Prophets of God.

— Bahá'u'lláh, *The Book of
Certitude* or *Kitáb-i-Íqán*, 38,
Bahá'í scripture)

Prayer's Blessings

There is nothing sweeter in the world of existence than
prayer. Man must live in a state of prayer. The most blessed
condition is the condition of prayer and supplication.
Prayer is conversation with God. The greatest attainment
or the sweetest state is none other than conversation with
God.

—'Abdu'l-Bahá (*Star of the West*,
vol. VIII, no. 4, May 17, 1917, 41)

Mystic Feelings

One's heart must be sensitive to the music of prayer. He must feel the effect of prayer. He must not be like an organ from which softest notes stream forth without having consciousness of sensation in itself.

—'Abdu'l-Bahá (*Star of the West*,
vol. VIII, no. 4, May 17, 1917, 41)

For the core of religious faith is that mystic feeling which unites Man with God. This state of spiritual communion can be brought about and maintained by means of meditation and prayer.

—Shoghi Effendi
(*Directives from the Guardian*, 86–87)

Spiritual Growth

Prayer and supplication are so effective that they inspire one's heart for the whole day with high ideals and supreme sanctity and calmness . . .

It creates spirituality, creates mindfulness and celestial feelings, begets new attractions of the Kingdom and engenders the susceptibilities of the higher intelligence . . .

—'Abdu'l-Bahá (*Star of the West*, vol.
VIII, no. 4, May 17, 1917, 41)

What is "Obligatory" Prayer?

> The wisdom of prayer is this: That it causeth a connection between the servant and the True One, because in that state (i.e., prayer) man with all heart and soul turneth his face towards His Highness the Almighty, seeking His association and desiring His love and compassion.
>
> —ʿABDUʾL-BAHÁ (*Tablets of ʿAbduʾl-Bahá*, v3, 683)

There are many times when circumstances in life motivate people to pray. In times of trouble, stress or illness, prayers are said to request divine assistance and protection. At moments of awe, prayers become a vehicle for expressing reverence and gratitude. Thanksgiving prayers may spring spontaneously from the heart. In contrast, obligatory prayer is the call to prayer daily, to remember God, regardless of the chances and changes of life.

For example, in Rabbinical Judaism, believers are instructed to pray daily, three times—morning, afternoon, and evenings. In Christian scripture there are many passages that call upon believers to pray (Matthew 5:44, 6:5, 6:9, Romans 12:12, Ephesians 6:18, Philippians 4:6, Colossians 4:2, 1 Thessalonians 5:17, 1 Timothy 2:1), as well as to pray regularly. One of the Five Pillars of Islam is the obligation to prayer daily.

The Baháʾí Faith continues this obligation to pray daily.

> Fasting and obligatory prayer are as two wings to man's life. Blessed be the one who soareth with their aid in the heaven of the love of God, the Lord of all worlds.
>
> —BAHÁʾUʾLLÁH (*The Importance of Obligatory Prayer and Fasting*, III)

Obligatory prayer is the very foundation of the Cause of God. Through it joy and vitality infuse the heart. Even if every grief should surround Me, as soon as I engage in conversing with God in obligatory prayer, all My sorrows disappear and I attain joy and gladness. A condition descendeth upon Me which I am unable to describe or express.

Whenever, with full awareness and humility, we undertake to perform the Obligatory Prayer before God, and recite it with heartfelt tenderness, we shall taste such sweetness as to endow all existence with eternal life.

—'Abdu'l-Bahá (*The Importance of Obligatory Prayer and Fasting*, XIV)

The Uniqueness of Bahá'í Obligatory Prayer

In addition to the obligation to pray daily, there are prayers revealed by Bahá'u'lláh to be used for that specific purpose. Among these obligatory prayers we find a wide range of prayer forms including praise, thanksgiving, lamentation, requests for aid, confession, testimony, reflection and invocation.

> The Bahá'í obligatory prayers are three in number. The shortest one consists of a single verse which is to be recited once in every twenty-four hours at midday. The medium (prayer) . . . is recited three times a day, in the morning, at noon and in the evening. The long prayer which is the most elaborate of the three is recited once in every twenty-four hours, at whatever time of day one feels inclined to do so.

The believer is entirely free to choose any one of those three prayers but is under the obligation of reciting one of them, and in accordance with any specific directions with which they may be accompanied. These daily obligatory prayers . . . have been invested by Bahá'u'lláh with a special potency and significance . . . that through them they may enter into a much closer communion with God . . .

—Shoghi Effendi (*Directives from the Guardian*, 60)

. . . in every word and movement of the Obligatory Prayer there are allusions, mysteries and a wisdom that man is unable to comprehend, and letters and scrolls cannot contain . . .

—'Abdu'l-Bahá (notes to the *Kitáb-i-Aqdas*, 167)

Of the three prayers—the short, the medium, and the long—this book explores the long prayer.

Long Obligatory Prayer

SECTION 1

O Thou Lord of All Names

لِلْمُصَلِّي أَنْ يَقُومَ مُقْبِلاً إِلَى اللّهِ وَإِذَا قَامَ وَاسْتَقَرَّ
فِي مَقَامِهِ يَنْظُرُ إِلَى الْيَمِينِ وَالشِّمَالِ كَمَنْ يَنْتَظِرُ
رَحْمَةَ رَبِّهِ الرَّحْمنِ الرَّحِيمِ ثُمَّ يَقُولُ:

TO BE RECITED ONCE IN
TWENTY-FOUR HOURS.

Whoso wisheth to recite this prayer, let him stand up and turn unto God and, as he standeth in his place, let him gaze to the right and to the left, as if awaiting the mercy of his Lord, the Most Merciful, the Compassionate. Then let him say:

O Thou Who art the Lord of all names and the Maker of the heavens! I beseech Thee by them Who are the Day-Springs of Thine invisible Essence, the Most Exalted, the All-Glorious, to make of my prayer a fire that will burn away the veils which have shut me out from Thy beauty, and a light that will lead me unto the ocean of Thy Presence.

Preparation enhances our prayer experience

"Whoso wisheth to recite this prayer" is broad language suggesting that the prayer is intended for any person who "wishes" to use it—no special class, station, or gender limitations are mentioned. "Recite" indicates that it is to be recited audibly, either from reading or from memory.

"Stand and turn" is a call to be reverent. It entails two simple actions. The first indicates a break from other activities, the second directing attention to a specific direction. Standing is the first prayer posture stipulated in the Long Obligatory Prayer. (See Prayer Postures, Section 2.)

"Turn to God" involves looking in a specific direction toward a holy place that is symbolic of the presence of God on earth. It is seen as a potent focus of divine energy. Historically, churches (Roman Catholic, Orthodox, and Anglican) were built facing east, the direction of Jerusalem and priests celebrated mass "ad orientem," meaning oriented to face Jerusalem. In Islam, Mecca is the "Qiblah," or direction for offering prayer. For Bahá'ís, the direction or Qiblah is Bahjí, Bahá'u'lláh's final resting place, situated in the traditional Holy Land of the Abrahamic faiths. For people living in North or South America, as well as much of Western Europe, this means facing generally eastwards, the direction of the sunrise.

> Facing in the direction of the Qiblih is a fixed requirement for the recitation of obligatory prayer, but for other prayers and devotions one may follow what the merciful Lord hath revealed in the Qur'án: "Whichever way ye turn, there is the face of God."
>
> —BAHÁ'U'LLÁH (*Kitáb-i-Aqdas*, 111)

"Gazing to the right and left" implies a search for God and a readiness to to move toward Him.

> If we are lovers of the light we adore it in whatever lamp it may become manifest . . . Therefore we must follow and adore the virtues revealed in the messengers of God whether in Abraham, Moses, Jesus or other prophets . . . We must recognize the sun no matter from what dawning-point it may shine forth . . . for we are lovers of sunlight . . .
>
> —'Abdu'l-Bahá (*The Promulgation of Universal Peace*, 152)

"Awaiting" demonstrates patience, an acknowledgement that we may not receive an immediate response. It involves both a willingness to accept delay and a desire to persevere in our effort to establish communion with God. In context: "Awaiting" represents the idea that we depend on God to guide us in His own time.

"Most Merciful," a superlative indicating that no one exceeds God in compassion. This awareness assures us of God's accessibility, making it easier for us to set aside fear and cultivate a heartfelt desire to maintain conscious contact with our Creator through prayer. There is much that can be attributed to God, such as power, potency, wisdom, but in this context "the Most Merciful, the Compassionate" emphasizes that God has compassionately and mercifully reached out to us to show us the way that is best for us. Now in prayer, we are reaching out to God in return to show that we are accepting and appreciating His mercy and compassion.

"Once in twenty-four hours." Although not explicitly stated, this instruction seems to imply that the prayer should be said each day. If a 24 hour period were to literally apply, one could not say

the prayer at 6 pm one day and 7 pm the next for that would be 25 hours. By observing the general tone of Bahá'u'lláh's commandments and the number of reasonable exceptions often made, we may have confidence that no troublesome literalness is intended.

O Thou . . .

"O" is in the vocative case. In modern English, "Thou" is used as a reverential and formal pronoun of address. By using, "Thou" instead of "You," the translator provides a literary way of acknowledging the station of Divinity as superior to ourselves. As worshippers preparing to commune with the Beloved, "O Thou" is a heart-felt plea, calling upon God to hear our prayer.

The seventeenth-century Christian philosopher, Blaise Pascal referred to a God-shaped vacuum in our hearts that can only be filled by the Creator. It is this void that we attempt to fill by time spent in prayer.

> Does the world seem gray with empty longing,
>
> Wearing every shade of cynical.
>
> And do you ever feel that There is something missing?
>
> The restless soul is searching.
>
> There's a god-shaped hole in all of us
>
> And it's a void only He can fill.
>
> —PLUMB (Popular Song)

"O" is the first sound in the chant "Om," (Sanscript: ॐ)used as a mantra in Hinduism, Buddhism and Jainism. The opening of the mouth, the larynx, the chest and the heart space are intended to make the worshipper more receptive to divine connection.

ॐ मणिपद्मे हूं

The popular sanscript mantra: Om mani padme hūm.

"O" may also be understood as a symbol of creation. The first jot of the first letter in the Holy Qur'án is a dot under the letter baa (ب) in the word bismillah, (meaning "in the name of God").

بسم الله

Bismillah, meaning "In the name of Allah." Arabic reads from right to left, same as Hebrew.

Among its many meanings, Primal Point may refer to this dot, understood to represent the first particle of creation. In modern astrophysical terms, it is comparable to the infinitely small cosmic egg of the Big Bang that exploded to form the stars and galaxies of the material universe. The shape of the letter "O" in our Latin alphabet can also be compared to waves of the expanding universe, hollow in the center and moving outward. Similarly our prayers generate vibrational energy that radiates into our surroundings.

"O" expands in amazement as we gain knowledge of the vastness of Creation and its infinite variety of physical forms, ranging from sub-atomic particles to atoms, molecules, plants, animals, landscapes, planets, stars, pulsars, quasars, galaxies, clusters, nebula and on and on. From a single point of first awareness, appreciation of the mystical nature of reality continually grows until every atom becomes a sign of God. Our awe and wonder is simply expressed by the exclamation "O."

Lord of All Names

In the context of references to God, the term "name" in the phrase "Lord of all names" can be taken to mean specific qualities attributed to God, such as God is the "Most Merciful" or the "Most Compassionate." It can also signify specific proper names or words used to identify entities, such as "Jehovah" derived from Hebrew scripture, or "Theos" used in the original Greek New Testament, or "deus" used in Latin translations, or "God" a Germanic word that first appears in Christian use in the 6th century, or "Allah" the Arabic word used in Arabic translations of the Bible by Christians since the 8th century in Arabic-speaking countries. "Allah" is, of course, also the word used in the Qur'án, the sacred book of Islam.

Too often people fight over religion, imagining that "my God" is different from or better than "their God." For many, the belief in One God is understood to mean that the diety worshipped by others is false and distinct from the only true God.

However, Bahá'í belief sees the seeming plurality of religions differently.

> That the divers communions of the earth, and the manifold systems of religious belief, should never be allowed to foster the feelings of animosity among men, is, in this Day, of the essence of the Faith of God and His Religion. These principles and laws, these firmly-established and mighty systems, have proceeded from one Source, and are rays of one Light.
>
> —BAHÁ'U'LLÁH (*Epistle to the Son of the Wolf*, 13)

When God calls Himself "Lord of All Names," the various divine names used by various cultures, peoples and faiths can be seen as properly belonging to the one true God who is creator of all. The various gods—Vishnu, Wakan Tanka, Jehovah, Allah—worshipped

in different religions are fused together, now seen as aspects or manifestations of the One God.

Names of God in Judaism

In the Hebrew Bible, God is most often referred to in Hebrew as יהוה (YHWH). The name is derived from the root word meaning "to be" and carries the meanings "self-existing," "self-sufficient" or, according to some scholars, "He who causes to be" (Creator). Christian Bibles sometimes translate the name as Yahweh or Jehovah, but Jews view the name as too sacred to pronounce. When the Torah is read in the synagogue, Adonai, meaning Lord, is read whenever יהוה is encountered in the text. Despite the distinction between what is written (ketiv) and what is read (qere), those hearing the reading understand that the sacred name is being invoked. Out of the same sense of reverence, Jews likewise often write "God" as "G-d," or refer to Him as Hashem, meaning the Name.

In ancient Israel, the surrounding Canaanite culture worshipped a proliferation of gods. The Bible mentions Baal—the god of storm and vegetation, El—the head of the pantheon, Ashtoreth —the goddess of fertility and Mo—the god of death among others. In advocating monotheism, the Bible writers apply the names and attributes of the Canaanite gods to the One God. Thus YHWH, as the Supreme God, is called El, Eloah, Elohim, El Shaddai, El Elyon and other variations rooted in the name El. YHWH likewise takes on the attributes of the god of fertility in Hannah's prayer (1 Samuel 1), the god of storm in Psalm 29 and the god of death in Psalm 139. Thus YHWH absorbs the names and attributes of El, Baal, Ashtoreth, Mot, etc.

At the same time, in advocating for the Most High God, the Bible prohibits the worship of the Canannite idol gods who are too limited or unsustainable to be worthy of God's transcendence. These lesser gods are gods in the sense of being objects of worship by individuals, tribes and nations, but do not merit such worship neither are they capable of fulfilling the needs of their worshippers.

The carpenter measures with a line
And makes an outline with a marker;
He roughs it out with chisels
And marks it with compasses.
He shapes it in human form,
Human form in all its glory,
That it may dwell in a shrine.
He cut down cedars . . .
Some of it he takes and warms himself,
He kindles a fire and bakes bread.
But he also fashions a god and worships it;
He makes an idol and bows down to it . . . .
He prays to it and says,
"Save me! You are my god!"
They know nothing, they understand nothing;
Their eyes are plastered over so they cannot see . . .
And their minds closed so they cannot understand.

(ISAIAH 44:13–17, Hebrew scripture)

Broadly speaking, the Hebrew term "shem" (name) is more than a label. The Jewish sages understood "names" to include the attributes of the LORD (YHWH). It encompasses His qualities and reputation. Thus "God's name" refers to all that is known of God, all characteristics, appellations, titles and descriptions. Drawn from the Torah text of Exodus 34, thirteen names of God are the subject of lengthy exposition by Talmudic and medieval scholars.

And the LORD descended in the cloud, and stood with him (Moses) there, and proclaimed the name of the LORD. And the LORD passed by before him, and proclaimed: 'The LORD, the LORD, God, merciful and gracious, slow to anger, and abundant in loving-kindness and

truth; keeping mercy unto the thousandth generation, forgiving transgression and sin and pardoning error . . .'
(EXODUS 34:5–7, HEBREW SCRIPTURE)

The thirteen attribute names are counted and interpreted as follows:

1. *Adonai* – the LORD showing compassion before a person sins;
2. *Adonai* – the LORD showing compassion after a person has sinned;
3. *El* – mighty in compassion fulfilling the needs of all creatures;
4. *Rachum* – merciful, that humankind may not be distressed;
5. *Chanun* – gracious if humankind is already in distress;
6. *Erech appayim* – slow to anger;
7. *Rav chesed* – abundant or great in loving-kindness;
8. *Emet* – truth;
9. *Notzer chesed laalafim* — showing mercy to thousands;
10. *Noseh avon* – forgiving iniquity;
11. *Noseh peshah* – forgiving transgression;
12. *Noseh chatah* – forgiving sin;
13. *Venakeh* – and pardoning error.

Yet there is no attempt to limit God to just these thirteen names. In specific contexts in the Hebrew Bible, a quality of God is singled out and used as His name.

For thou shalt worship no other gods: for YHWH, whose name is Jealous, is a jealous God: (EXODUS 34:14, Hebrew scripture)

In Kabbalah, a late Jewish mystical discipline, the Hebrew letters of Exodus 14:19–21 are rearranged by aligning parallel verses to derive 72 names of God. Recitation of the 72 names is said to bring abundance of blessings prosperity and happiness.

In conclusion, we can see that in Judaism, the divine name is prominently associated with the appellation YHWH, but also includes a multiplicity of additional names and qualities of God. Throughout Israel's history, the list of names of God has grown to reflect the continued revelation of God's nature as it becomes apparent in His interactions with His people.

> Like other Hebrew proper names, the name of God is more than a mere distinguishing title . . . It represents the Deity as He is known to His worshipers, and stands for all those attributes which He bears in relation to them and which are revealed to them through His activity on their behalf. A new manifestation of His interest or care may give rise to a new name. (*Jewish Encyclopedia*, 1906, "Names of God")

Names of God in Christian usage

Early Christians used the Greek translation of the Hebrew Bible, known as the *Septuagint*. This Jewish translation retained the practice of writing God's name יהוה (called the tetragrammaton, meaning four letters) wherever that name appeared in the original Hebrew. According to the third-century writer, Origen Adamantius, some Christians mistook the Hebrew יהוה for the Greek Π Ι Π Ι and began pronouncing the Name as "Pipi." To avoid this confusion, later Christian Greek versions of the Old Testament replaced the tetragrammaton with the Greek theos (God) or kyrios (Lord), in accord with the Jewish oral reading custom. These are the words used in Greek literature to refer to the gods, such as those mentioned in the Homer's Iliad and Odyssey.

The Latin Vulgate, translated by St. Jerome in the fourth century C.E., became the standard Bible of the Roman Catholic Church. From the beginning, the Vulgate omitted YHWH in favor of Deus and Dominus, the Latin words from which English derives "diety" and "dominion."

Despite the removal of YHWH from official Church-sponsored translations of the Old Testament, remnants of the Hebrew name of God remained. The shortened form "Jah" is found in the phrase "Hallelujah" and in theophoric names, such as Johnathan and Jehu. Some English translations use the forms "Jehovah" or "Yahweh" to represent the Hebrew original.

During the early Christian era, YHWH was used in magical texts. Anyone who knew the correct pronunciation of the name was thought to have supernatural powers for healing and performing miracles, enhancing the mystery surrounding the sacred name.

Although Christian denominations vary as to their treatment and usage of YHWH. Seldom is the Hebrew name of God used. A more commonly invocation is the triune call, "in the name of the Father, the Son and the Holy Spirit." Here name is not intended to signify a particular appellation., for clearly the Holy Spirit is never given a personal name. Just as we might say "open up in the name of the law," "in the name of" refers to the power and supremacy of an authority, rather than a specific personal name.

> Our Father which art in heaven, Hallowed be thy name.
>
> —JESUS CHRIST (MATTHEW 6:10,
> Christian scripture)

> . . . baptizing them in the name of the Father, and of the Son, and of the Holy Spirit . . .
>
> —JESUS CHRIST (MATTHEW 28:19,
> Christian scripture)

> For as I passed by, and beheld your devotions, I found an altar with this inscription, to the Unknown God. Whom therefore ye ignorantly worship, him declare I unto you.
>
> —SAINT PAUL (ACTS 17:23,
> St. Paul to the men of
> Athens, Christian scripture)

Names of God in Islám

> To Him belong the Most Beautiful Names: whatever is
> in the heavens and on earth, doth declare His Praises and
> Glory . . .
>
> —Qur'án (Surah 59:24,
> Islámic scripture)

> Say: Call upon God or call upon the All-Merciful: by
> whichsoever name ye will invoke him, for He hath most
> excellent names.
>
> —Qur'án (Surah 17:110,
> Islámic scripture)

Allah is the most frequently used name of God in Islám. It is an
Arabic word meaning "the God." Allah is related to the Hebrew
names Eloah and Elohim. The name al-Qayyum (the Self-Subsisting) corresponds in meaning to the Hebrew name of God, YHWH.
In the Qur'án, the names Living and Self-Subsistent are linked. To
be alive is to exist.

> God, there is no god but He, the living, the self-subsistent.
>
> —Qur'án (Surah 2:255,
> Islámic scripture)

In Islámic tradition, God is said to have 99 names and attributes,
each laden with spiritual power. Chanting the names brings special
blessings.

> There are ninety-nine names of God. Whoever believes in
> their meanings and acts accordingly will enter Paradise.
>
> —Hadith (Abu Hurairah,
> *Sahih Bukhari*, Book 75:419,
> Islámic tradition)

Various Qur'ánic scholars who interpreted "99" literally have attempted to compile definitive lists of the 99 names. While there is general agreement on the more commonly used names, considerable variations exist regarding which of the lesser used forms should be counted among the 99.

> With us, the name of everything is its outward appearance;
> With the Creator, the name of each thing is its inward
>   reality.
> In the eye of Moses, the name of his rod was "staff";
> In the eye of the Creator, its name was "dragon."
> —JALALUDDIN RUMI,
> (*Mathnawi* I:1239–40,
> Islámic poet)

Arabic calligraphy: "Allah."

Selected names in Islám from Qur'án

ARABIC NAME	TRANSLATION	VERSE IN QUR'ÁN
Rahman	Beneficent	1:1
Rahim	Merciful	1:1
Malik	King	59:23
Quddus	Holy	59:23
Salam	Source of Peace	59:23
Mu'min	Granter	59:23
Muhaymin	Guardian	59:23
'Aziz	Almighty	59:23
Khaliq	Creator	59:24
Hayy	Living	2:255
Qayyum	Self-Subsisting	2:255

Hindu beliefs and practices invoking the names of God

> I manifest for thee those hundred thousand thousand
> shapes that clothe my Mystery . . .
>
> —Krishna (Bhagavad Gita,
> chapter XI, Hindu scripture)

In Hinduism, the various "shapes" of God are designated by names such as: Brahma, Vishnu, Kali, Rama, etc. They are often referred to as separate gods, but when one digs into underlying Hindu beliefs, it becomes apparent that the various gods are understood to be ema-nations, manifestations or aspects of the one overarching Supreme Deity.

> He said, and asked again: 'How many gods are there really,
>   O Yagnavalkya?
> 'One,' he said.
> 'Yes,' he said, and asked:
> 'Who are these three and three hundred, three and three
>   thousand?'
> Yagnavalkya replied: 'They are only the various powers of
>   them . . ."
>
> (Brihadaranyaka Upanishad 3.9.1,
> Hindu scripture)

As in many other traditions, recitation of the names of God is a sacred practice of special potency and blessing.

> Verily nothing is more purifying than the holy name of
> God.
>
> —Sukadeva Gosvami (Srimad
> Bhagavatam 6.1, Hindu scripture)

In Hindu practice, lists of 1000 names, called sahasranamas, are chanted daily. The Vishnu Sahasranama is one of the most popular. Interestingly, names of other "deities" such as Brahma and Shiva are found in all such lists indicating that the divergent names are seen as applicable to the One all-encompassing God. The chanting of Vishnu's names is said to produce phonetic vibrations which cleanse the mind and aid in the liberation of the soul. The conclusion of the hymn encourages and explains the benefits of recitation of God's many names, yet the names are stated as belonging to a singular "Lotus-Eyed One."

> One who reads this hymn every day with devotion and attention attains to peace of mind, patience, prosperity, mental stability, memory and reputation . . . . Whoever desires advancement and happiness should repeat this devotional hymn on Vishnu . . . . Never will defeat attend on a man who adores the Lotus-Eyed One, who is the Master of all the worlds, who is birthless, and out of whom the worlds have originated and into whom they dissolve.
> —HINDU HYMN
> (Vishnu Sahasranama)

Selected Hindu Divine Names

Sanskrit Name	Translation
Ganesha	Lord of All
Shiva	Auspicious, Kind
Vishnu	Omnipresent
Bhoota-Bhavya-Bhavat-Prabhuh	Past-Future-Present-Lord
Brahma	Creator
Bhoota-Bhrid	Sustainer
Bhaavo	Eternal
Bhootaatmaa	Universal Soul
Bhootabhaavanah	Universal Nourisher
Vashhathkaaro	Sovereign
Vishvam	All Existent

A World Embracing Vision of Divine Names

Belief in God or unseen spiritual powers is a universal human trait. Virtually all ancient peoples held a concept of a Creator deity, a Great Spirit who was responsible for making the earth and subsequently entitled to rule it as Lord of All. At times the Creator was initially seen as head of a pantheon, but, as time wore on, the figure of the Creator took on the character of the chief or only God who held people morally accountable for their actions.

There are certain exceptions, traditions and cultures that lack similar theistic terminology, but these hold to spiritual beliefs and use alternative language to refer to what others would call God or gods. Confucianism, for example, uses Heaven to speak of spiritual forces. Dharmakaya is the corresponding term in Buddhism. A sense of reverence for forces greater than humanity is intrinsic to human nature, found in every tribe and people in every geographic region and every age of the world. Just as Roman Catholics pray to God, Jesus, or the many Catholic saints, some Buddhist pray to Buddha or the many saints known as Bodhisattvas.

Selected Worldwide Divine Names

DIVINE NAME	MEANING OR STATION	ORIGIN
Aten	Source of Life in the Sun	Egypt, North Africa
Kwoth nhiali	High God	Nuer, Sudan, Africa
Chukwu	High God	Ibo, Nigeria, Africa
Nyasi	High God	Luo, Kenya, Africa
Leza	High God	Baila, Zambia, Africa
Mvelincanti	The One Who Came	Swazi, South Africa
Taronhiawagon	He Who Holds Up the	Iroquois, North America
Wakhan Thanka	Almighty Mystery	Lakota, North America
Gichi Manidoo	Great Spirit	Ojibwe, North America
Quetzalcoatl	Feathered Serpent	Mexico, North America
Ahaw	Lord	Maya, Central America
Inti	Chief God, Sun God	Inca, South America
Ahura Mazda	Light Wisdom (Creator)	Persia, Asia
Karta Purakh	Creator	Punjab, Asia
Tian	Source of the Cosmos	China, Asia
Cao Dai	Highest Lord	Vietnam, Asia
Kami Musubi No Kami	Divine Producing Deity	Japan, Asia
Bathala	Creator of the first	Philippines, Asia
Ranginui	Sky Father	Polynesia

Names of God in Bahá'í Belief and Practice

The designation "Lord of All Names" points to the myriad of names, titles, descriptions and attributes of God as used in the sacred books and oral traditions of all religions. It encompasses divine names from all parts of the earth, in every age, language and culture, even those of ages past, long forgotten, making it impossible to compile a comprehensive list of all names. The Bahá'í Writings accordingly recognize "infinite Divine Names and Attributes" (*Kitáb-i-Aqdas*, 176) for the Universal Reality who is Creator of All Worlds.

Many of the sacred names, descriptions and terminology found in the books of previous dispensations are specifically cited and affirmed in Bahá'í Writings, be they from the Hebrew Bible, the Christian New Testament or the Holy Qur'án.

> Jehovah is a title of God, whereas Bahá'u'lláh is the title of the Manifestation of God. (SHOGHI EFFENDI, *The Unfolding Destiny of the British Bahá'í Community*, 432)

> The Lord God Omnipotent hath been enthroned in His Kingdom and hath made all things new. This is the truth and what truth can be greater than that announced by the Revelation of St. John the Divine? He is Alpha and Omega. He is the One that will give unto him that is athirst of the fountain of the water of life and bestow upon the sick the remedy of true salvation. (*Selections from the Writings of 'Abdu'l-Bahá*, 12)

> 'Allah is the light of the Heavens, and of the Earth'. ('ABDU'L-BAHÁ QUOTING THE QUR'ÁN, *Paris Talks*, 69)

Recitation of the name of God is a Bahá'í meditative practice described in the *Kitáb-i-Aqdas*.

> It hath been ordained that every believer in God . . . shall, each day . . . repeat "Alláh-u-Abhá" ninety-five times.

"Alláh-u-Abhá" is an Arabic phrase meaning "God, the
All-Glorious" . . . (*Notes to the Kitáb-i-Aqdas,* 179)

In addition, Bahá'ís use an uncounted number of attributes of God
as names, The Long Healing Prayer alone contains at least 128 names
which serve as an invocation and a prelude to the specific petition
for healing which occurs toward the end of the prayer. The names
are grouped in threes with a repetitive refrain of the following form:

> I call on Thee O Sovereign, O Upraiser, O Judge! Thou the
> Sufficing, Thou the Healing, Thou the Abiding, O Thou
> Abiding One! . . . (*Bahá'í Prayers,* 102)

The essence of Bahá'í belief is the unity of God. It affirms that what
appear to be separate systems of worship are actually parts of one
overarching spiritual enterprise. "This is the changeless Faith of
God, eternal in the past, eternal in the future." (Bahá'u'lláh, *Kitáb-i-
Aqdas,* 85) The use of infinite names for the One object of universal
adoration, including those common to other faith traditions, reflects
that basic tenet.

> . . . in Divinity there is no duality. All adjectives, nouns
> and pronouns in that court of sanctity are one; there is nei-
> ther multiplicity nor division. ('ABDU'L-BAHÁ, *The Promul-
> gation of Universal Peace,* 155)

> I implore Thee, O Thou Maker of the heavens and Lord
> of all names . . . to send down upon Thy loved ones that
> which will draw them nearer unto Thee . . . (*Prayers and
> Meditations by Bahá'u'lláh,* 7)

Selected Bahá'í Divine Names

DIVINE NAMES AND ATTRIBUTES	REFERENCE IN BAHÁ'Í WRITINGS
God	Short Obligatory Prayer
The Help in Peril	Short Obligatory Prayer
The Self-Subsisting	Short Obligatory Prayer
Almighty	Medium Obligatory Prayer
Lord	Medium Obligatory Prayer
Most Merciful	Medium Obligatory Prayer
Ever-Forgiving	Medium Obligatory Prayer
Lord of All Names	Long Obligatory Prayer
Maker of the Heavens	Long Obligatory Prayer
Desire of the World	Long Obligatory Prayer
All-Glorious	Long Obligatory Prayer
Most High	Long Obligatory Prayer
King	Long Obligatory Prayer
All-Knowing	Long Obligatory Prayer
Lord of All Being	Long Obligatory Prayer
Lord of the Worlds	Long Obligatory Prayer
Sufficer	Long Healing Prayer
Healer	Long Healing Prayer
Abider	Long Healing Prayer
God of Grace to the Wicked	Long Healing Prayer

Maker of the heavens!

"Maker" is, of course, a synonym for "Creator." Here, our prayer calls on God by one of His best-known names, acknowledging Him as the One who brought the heavens into being.

Why not also "Maker of the earth?"

If the purpose were merely to praise God as Creator, we might well expect that other of God's creative works would be mentioned. Why is heaven singled out? The height of heaven, and its synonym sky make them appropriate symbols for what is lofty, spiritual. Our attention is being directed upward.

What are the various meanings of "heaven?"

In world scripture, of both Abrahamic and non-Abrahamic traditions, the term heaven carries both a physical meaning as well as a variety of spiritual meanings.

1. In terms of what we see with our naked eyes, our world is composed of two halves, upper and lower. The phrase "heaven and earth" thus represents the entire physical universe. In its physical sense, heaven refers to that upper part of the visible world, all that is above the horizon. As such, it forms a complement to the "earth," the lower half of our world, containing mountains, valleys, seas and rivers. The physical heavens have two levels, the atmosphere as the abode of winds, clouds and birds, and what we have come to call outer space, the abode of the sun, stars, and heavenly bodies.

> . . . birds that fly above the earth in the open firmament of heaven. (Genesis 1:20, Hebrew scripture)

> Space, star-sprinkled and void place, From pole to pole of the Blue! (Bhagavad Gita, Chapter XI, Hindu scripture)

. . . it has been established by science that the material
heaven is a limitless space, void and empty, wherein count-
less stars and planets move ('ABDU'L-BAHÁ, *Some Answered
Questions*, 23, 5)

2. By contrast, the invisible heavens are the seat of spiritual
things. Accordingly, God is said to be "in heaven" and God's
blessings descend from "heaven."

Our Father which art in heaven. (MATTHEW 6:9, CHRIS-
TIAN SCRIPTURE)

This is the springtime of manifestation. The vernal
shower has descended from the cloud of divine mercy . . .
('ABDU'L-BAHÁ, *The Promulgation of Universal Peace*, 210)

This spiritual heaven is not a location up in the sky but is "higher"
than anything material beings ever could perceive. In order to
express the relationship between the material and the spiritual, the
sacred writings use the attributes of the visible heavens as symbols;
clouds, birds, the sun, the horizon, the moon, stars come to represent spiritual realities that are unseen, invisible. Just as the physical
sky is illuminated by sun, moon, and stars whose light litters the sky,
so too the spiritual heavens provide Divine guidance which shines
down over every part of our planet. And clouds become symbols of
any obstacle that blocks divine light.

"For the LORD God is a sun . . ." (PSALM 84:11, Hebrew
scripture)

. . . the Essence of Divinity, the Sun of Truth, shines forth
upon all horizons and is spreading its rays upon all things.
Each creature is the recipient of some portion of that power
. . . (*'Abdu'l-Bah in London*, 23)

But when He (Christ) declared that He had come from
Heaven, it is clear that He did not mean the blue firma-

ment but that He spoke of the Heaven of the Kingdom of God, and that from this Heaven He descended upon the clouds. As clouds are obstacles to the shining of the sun, so the clouds of the world of humanity hid from the eyes of men the radiance of the Divinity of Christ. ('ABDU'L-BAHÁ, *Paris Talks*, 43–4)

3. In addition to comparing all the physical attributes of the sky to spiritual things, the sacred writings also describe God as being above heaven. This usage indicates the infinite, unapproachable, incomprehensible aspect of divinity.

> Too high art Thou exalted for . . . the understanding of any heart to scale the heights of Thine immeasurable knowledge. (BAHÁ'U'LLÁH, *Prayers and Meditations*, 88)

> High is His Heavenly Home.
> Highest of the High, above all is His Name.
> Only one as Great and as High as God
> Can know His Lofty and Exalted State.
> Only He Himself is that Great.
> He Himself knows Himself.
> (SHRI GURU GRANT SAHIB, Section 1 – Jup – Part 5, Sikh scripture)

> . . . the only Potentate, the King of kings, and Lord of lords; Who only hath immortality, dwelling in the light which no man can approach . . . (1 TIMOTHY 6:15–16, Christian scripture)

When King Solomon was dedicating the Jerusalem Temple, he made clear that the Almighty could not be restricted to one building, no matter how large or luxurious. The Temple was to be a symbolic residence of God, not his actual abode. In Solomon's language, there is a heaven, a heaven above the heavens and, ultimately, a divine realm still higher yet.

But will God indeed dwell on the earth? Behold, the heaven and heaven of heavens cannot contain thee; how much less this House that I have built? (1 KINGS 8:27, Hebrew scripture)

4. Like the rays of the heavenly sun that shed their light upon the earth, spiritual virtues that originate with God are said to be heavenly, although they exist on earth among humanity. Thus heaven and earth are united by divine light.

> To Thee alone belongs to tell the heavenly excellence
> Of those perfections wherewith Thou dost fill these worlds
>   of Thine;
> Pervading, Immanent! (BHAGAVAD GITA, Chapter X,
>   Hindu scripture)

5. A key to one of the deeper meanings hidden in the term "heaven" is its reference to the place of the origin of sacred books.

> . . . the heaven of the Revelation of Him Who is the Lord of Religions . . . (BAHÁ'U'LLÁH, *Epistle to the Son of the Wolf*, 79)
>
> . . . the heaven of every religion . . . (BAHÁ'U'LLÁH, *Kitáb-i-Aqdas*, 21)

How unifying it is that one of the names of God is "Lord of Religions." Thus, when God is called "Maker of the Heavens," it is not only in reference to the creation of the visible sky. He is also being credited as the Founder of Religion, the faiths of all the peoples, cultures and ages of history. Divine revelation proceeds from His lofty heavenly throne, outside of time and space, shedding its light throughout the ages into every corner of our planet.

The advent of each new Revelation, in this sense, brings an end and a fresh beginning, a "new heaven and a new earth," with new spiritual insights, new laws, new institutions and a reborn body of believers.

> And all the host of heaven shall be dissolved, and the heavens shall be rolled together as a scroll: and all their host shall fall down . . . (ISAIAH 34:4, Hebrew scripture)

> For, behold, I create new heavens and a new earth . . . (ISAIAH 65:17, Hebrew scripture)

> . . . reflect how the elevated heavens of the Dispensations of the past have, in the right hand of power, been folded together, how the heavens of divine Revelation have been raised by the command of God, and been adorned by the sun, the moon, and stars of His wondrous commandments. (BAHÁ'U'LLÁH, *Kitáb-i-Íqán*, 48)

> . . . so that they, too, may become a new people . . . may make the world a new world, to the end that the old earth may disappear and the new earth appear; old ideas depart and new thoughts come; old garments be cast aside and new garments put on; ancient politics whose foundation is war be discarded and modern politics founded on peace raise the standard of victory . . . ('ABDU'L-BAHÁ, *Tablets of 'Abdu'l-Bahá*, vol. 1, 38)

The religions of the world are different in belief and practice. How could One God be Maker of them all?

> The ocean is one body of water, but different parts of it have particular designations—Atlantic, Pacific, Mediterranean, Antarctic, etc. If we consider the names, there is differentiation; but the water, the ocean itself, is one reality.
> Likewise, the divine religions of the holy Manifestations of God are in reality one, though in name . . . they differ. ('ABDU'L-BAHÁ, *The Promulgation of Universal Peace*, 151)

The religion of God consists of two parts: One is the very
foundation and belongs to the spiritual realm; that is,
it pertains to spiritual virtues and divine qualities. This
part suffers neither change nor alteration: It is the Holy
of Holies, which constitutes the essence of the religion of
Adam, Noah, Abraham, Moses, Christ, Muhammad, the
Báb, and Bahá'u'lláh, and which will endure throughout
all the prophetic Dispensations. It will never be abrogated,
for it consists in spiritual rather than material truth. It is
faith, knowledge, certitude, justice, piety, high-minded-
ness, trustworthiness, love of God, and charity. It is mercy
to the poor, assistance to the oppressed, generosity to the
needy, and upliftment of the fallen . . .

The second part of the religion of God, which pertains
to the material world and which concerns such things as
fasting; prayer; worship; marriage; divorce; manumission;
legal rulings; transactions; and penalties and punishments
for murder, assault, theft, and injury, is changed and altered
in every prophetic Dispensation and may be abrogated—
for policies, transactions, punishments, and other laws are
bound to change according to the exigencies of the time.
('ABDU'L-BAHÁ, *Some Answered Questions*, 11, 7 and 10)

How can the various symbols of the Prophets of God as sources
of light be sorted out? Sometimes the metaphor of heavenly lights
is mixed with metaphors of man-made lights, such as lamps, fire
or candles. The use of various light source images is not, however,
intended to indicate that one is brighter, more luminous or greater
than the other, but simply that all are sources of light using images
common to the various spiritual books. Thus, in the Bible, Christ
is compared to the morning star, the planet Venus, which appears
prophetically as a sign of the coming of a New Day (Revelation
22:16 as quoted above), and, in the Bahá'í Writings, He is compared to the much brighter Sun as a Manifestation of Divine Light.

('Abdu'l-Bahá, Paris Talks, 21) Similarly, each of the Prophets can be described as being a particular symbol of light, with no intent to make one Prophet brighter or better than another.

> Blessed souls—whether Moses, Jesus, Zoroaster, Krishna, Buddha, Confucius or Muhammad—were the cause of the illumination of the world of humanity . . . The light of Christ is evident. The candle of Buddha is shining. The star of Moses is sparkling. The flame ignited by Zoroaster is still burning. How can we deny Them? ('ABDU'L-BAHÁ, *The Promulgation of Universal Peace*, 346)

I beseech Thee . . .

The Long Obligatory Prayer contains numerous requests for divine assistance. To beseech is to petition or to make a request with emotional intensity. As one who would humbly come before the throne of a King, a lowly attitude acknowledges the authority of our Creator to either grant or deny our request. Its emphatic tone emphasizes our longing, our yearning, our deep hunger to have our prayer heard. The supplicant makes a humble request before the majesty of the Creator.

Several synonymous terms are found in this prayer related to making requests of God. In addition to "beseech," we find "beg," "entreat" and "implore."

In many of Bahá'u'lláh's prayers, we often find a specific petition format.

- A personalized address to the Divine: . . . "O my God . . ."

- An invocation that sanctifies the request by calling upon the merits of something holy, such as an attribute of God or His Manifestations. It sets a reverential tone and prepares the ground for the coming request. Often, the invocation uses a metaphor of praise, such as ". . . by Thy Beauty that shineth forth above the horizon of eternity, a Beauty before which as soon as it revealeth itself the kingdom of beauty boweth down in worship, magnifying it in ringing tones . . ."

- The specific request such as, "to grant that I may die to all that I possess and live to whatsoever belongeth unto Thee."

- A closing that again acknowledges divine authority by reciting one or more of God's Holy Names, such as . . . . "There is no God but Thee, the All-Knowing, the All-Wise."

In addition to petitions, scholars categorize prayer into several over-lapping types. There are prayers of praise, prayers of personal or communal lamentation, and supplications for assistence, which can include both requests for material help or for spiritual gain, such as a desire to grow in awareness of the divine presence. All of these types of prayer expression are found numerous times scattered through the various sections of the Long Obligatory Prayer.

. . . *Daysprings of Thine invisible Essence* . . .

What are "Daysprings?" The light of day, as it first appears at dawn, is referred to as a dayspring. When the Prophets of God come into the world, they are bearers of new light and are therefore fittingly called Daysprings.

> Thus, it hath become evident that the terms "sun," "moon," and "stars" primarily signify the Prophets of God, the saints, and their companions, those Luminaries, the light of Whose knowledge hath shed illumination upon the worlds of the visible and the invisible. (Bahá'u'lláh, *Kitáb-i-Íqán*, 35)

These divine Messengers carry distinct revelations adapted to the needs of their age. The differences between the various revelations are compared to the compass points on the horizon where the sun first appears depending on the time of year, whether due east, northeast or southeast.

> The Sun of Reality is one Sun, but it has different dawning places, just as the phenomenal sun is one although it appears at various points of the horizon. During the time of summer the luminary of the physical world rises far to the north of the equinoctial, in spring and fall it dawns midway, and in winter it appears in the most southerly point of its zodiacal journey. ('Abdu'l-Bahá, *The Promulgation of Universal Peace*, 94)

> The holy Manifestations Who have been the Sources or Founders of the various religious systems were united and agreed in purpose and teaching. Abraham, Moses, Zoroaster, Buddha, Jesus, Muhammad, the Báb and Bahá'u'lláh are one in spirit and reality. ('Abdu'l-Bahá, *The Promulgation of Universal Peace*, 197)

Why is the symbolism of "Daysprings" appropriate to the Prophets?

The Prophets of God, like the dawn of a new day, bring new spiritual light into the darkness of a world alienated from its Creator.

> . . . . the Sun of Truth at one time shed its rays from the sign of Abraham; later it dawned above the sign of Moses and illumined the horizon; and later still it shone forth with the utmost power, heat, and radiance from the sign of Christ . . . . Therefore one must search after truth, become enraptured and enthralled with any sanctified soul in whom one finds it, and become wholly attracted to the outpouring grace of God. Like a moth, one must be a lover of the light, in whatever lamp it may shine . . . ('ABDU'L-BAHÁ, *Some Answered Questions*, 14, 13–14)

> . . . When the Sun of Reality returns to quicken the world of mankind, a divine bounty descends from the heaven of generosity. The realm of thoughts and ideals is set in motion and blessed with new life. Minds are developed, hopes brighten, aspirations become spiritual, the virtues of the human world appear with freshened power of growth and the image and likeness of God become visible in man. It is the springtime of the inner world. ('ABDU'L-BAHÁ, *Foundations of World Unity*, 11)

What is the significance of there being more than one "Day-Spring?"

Just as the dawn reoccurs in regular daily cycles, the appearances of the Prophets of God occur to usher in each age of the world.

> Manifold the renewals of my birth . . .

Albeit I be unborn, undying, indestructible,
The Lord of all things living . . .
On floating Nature-forms, the primal vast-
I come, and go, and come.
When Righteousness declines . . .
When Wickedness is strong,
I rise, from age to age,
And take visible shape,
And move (as) a man with men,
Succoring the good, thrusting the evil back,
And setting Virtue on her seat again.

(BHAGAVAD GITA 4:5–8, *Saying of Krishna,*
 Hindu scripture)

I go away, and come again unto you. (JOHN 14:28, *Saying of Jesus, Christian scripture*)

Moreover He hath in every age and cycle, in conformity with His transcendent wisdom, sent forth a divine Messenger to revive the dispirited and despondent souls . . . (*Tablets of Bahá'u'lláh*, 161)

The marvelous bestowals of God are continuous. Should the outpouring of light be suspended, we would be in darkness. But how could it be withheld? If the divine graces are suspended, then divinity itself would be interrupted . . . and leave us deprived of the sun's bestowals which are the wisdom and guidance of God and the favor of God, which constitute spiritual progress. (REPORTED BY ISABEL FRASER CHAMBERLAIN AS A QUOTE FROM 'ABDU'L-BAHÁ, *Divine Philosophy*, 34)

What is meant by God's "invisible essence?"

The essence of God's being is of a higher order of being, invisible, beyond human comprehension. God is known indirectly through His works of creation and the spiritual light of His Word, which reaches the world through His "Daysprings."

> The pictures of Divinity that come to our mind are the product of our fancy; they exist in the realm of our imagination. They are not adequate to the Truth; truth in its essence cannot be put into words . . . . But the Essence of Divinity, the Sun of Truth, shines forth upon all horizons and is spreading its rays upon all things. (*'Abdu'l-Bahá in London*, 22)

> All comforts and peace, and the Essence of the Lord, are enjoyed by acquiring spiritual wisdom in Fellowship with the Saints. (SHRI GURU GRANTH SAHIB, Section 5 – Siree Raag, Sikh scripture)

... *the Most Exalted,*
the All-Glorious ...

"Exalted" signifies "elevated in rank, character or status." Physical height is used as an analogy for a spiritual station. Most Exalted, as a name of God, is a superlative form. "Most" signifies that God represents the highest possible order of existence, far above all other things, material and spiritual. The Divine station is infinitely above our own, a gulf too wide to bridge.

> Too high art Thou exalted for the eye of any creature to behold Thy beauty, or for the understanding of any heart to scale the heights of Thine immeasurable knowledge. (BAHÁ'U'LLÁH, *Prayers and Meditations*, 88)

> (God) is the blessed and only Potentate, the King of kings, and Lord of lords; Who only hath immortality, dwelling in the light which no man can approach; whom no man hath seen, nor can see . . . (1 TIMOTHY 6:15–16, Christian scripture)

This lack of approachability helps explain the difficulty humans have in understanding the Nature of God. God is an unknowable essence. His attributes can only be partially glimpsed in the revelation of His Prophets.

> God . . . (has) spoken unto us by his Son, whom he hath appointed heir of all things, by whom also he made the worlds; Who is the brightness of His glory, and the express image of his person . . . (HEBREWS 1:1–3, Christian scripture)

Humans, as contingent, finite beings, can never comprehend the infinite. The Ultimate Being exists in a state of Reality that we have no way of grasping.

The Prayer couples "Glory" with "Exalted," forming a natural pair. Together they signify the height of honor, beauty, and splendor. "All-Glorious" is a superlative that indicates the highest degree of glory, more majestic than the most elegant throne room of history's greatest King, brighter than the most brilliant sun.

> The Quintessence of Glory hath lifted up its voice above My head, and crieth from such heights as neither pen nor tongue can in any degree describe . . . (*Gleanings from the Writings of Bahá'u'lláh*, 36)

God's superlative exaltation and glory motivate us in our ongoing search to increase our closeness to God. The faintest glimmer of Divinity is so awesome it make worthwhile every effort to reach for this noblest and most rewarding of goals.

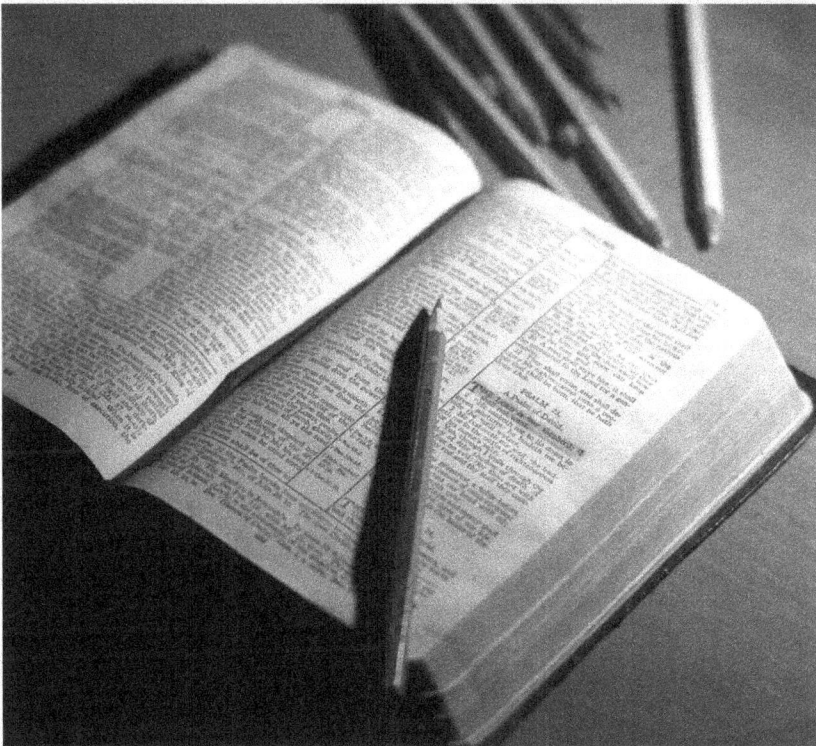

. . . to make of my prayer a fire that will burn away the veils . . .

After the words of the prayer have oriented us to God, we now reach the first request of the Prayer. We make a specific request that God remove the obstacles that hinder us from attaining a closer communion. These obstacles are referred to as veils that we ask God to "burn away,"

A closer look at "veils?"

Just as a cloud might block the sun or a window curtain hide the interior of a house, veils are a metaphor used in sacred writings to refer to whatever hinders our vision and prevents us from experiencing the divine.

> Consider the radiant glory of the great solar center of our planetary system (the Sun): how wonderful the sight, how its splendor illumines vision until clouds and mists veil it from the eye. In the same way, the Sun of Truth becomes veiled and hidden by the superstitions and imaginations of human minds. ('ABDU'L-BAHÁ, *The Promulgation of Universal Peace,* 78)

In the Jerusalem Temple, the innermost chamber was called the Holy of Holies (or Most Holy). It represented the presence of God. This was the place in the Temple that contained the sacred Ark of the Covenant, (the symbolic Throne of God), protected on either side by cherubs with outstretched wings. Hovering between the wings hovered the miraculous Shekinah light, a visible representation of the invisible God.

A curtain separated this Most Holy spot from the rest of the Temple, veiling God's sacred presence. The High Priest would pass

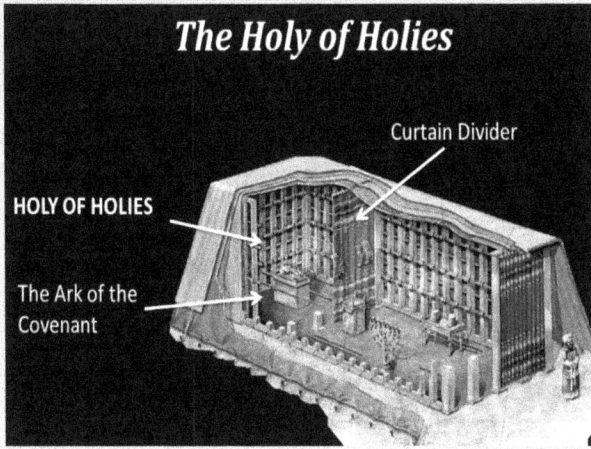

The Holy of Holies

through the curtain once a year on the Day of Atonement to offer sacrifices for the sins of the people.

According to Christian scripture, the veil was miraculously torn asunder at the moment of Jesus' death. Just as the curtain represented separation from God, its removal symbolized the removal of barriers between humanity and God.

> Jesus, when he had cried again with a loud voice, yielded up His spirit. And, behold, the veil of the temple was rent in two from top to bottom . . . (MATTHEW 27:50–51, Christian scripture)

> Which hope we have as an anchor of the soul, both sure and steadfast, and which enters within the veil; where a forerunner has already entered on our behalf, even Jesus, made a high priest . . . (HEBREWS 6:19–20, Christian scripture)

Veil imagery

In the east, women are customarily "veiled" in public as a sign of modesty, so that their beauty does not draw unwanted attention. According to various customs depending on times and places, the body, the legs, the hair and/or even the face are veiled with special clothing. Only husbands, fathers and other male family members are allowed to see women unveiled. In large households, the women are often separated from men in a special part of the house, called a harem or purdah. The curtain over the entrance to the harem is likewise referred to as a veil.

In sacred literature, the veil is used in a wide variety of contexts as a symbol of restrictions on drawing closer to God.

> Hard it is to pierce that veil divine of various disguises
>   which hideth Me;
> Yet they who worship Me pierce it and pass beyond.
>   (KRISHNA, BHAGAVAD GITA, VII, Hindu scripture)

> But our Gospel is veiled . . . ., so that the glorious good news of Christ, who is the image of God, might not shine through. (2 CORINTHIANS 4:4, Christian scripture)

> Past and future are what veil God from our sight. Burn up both of them with fire! (RUMI, MATHNAVI, VOL 1, STORY VIII, ISLÁMIC POET)

> Tear off the obstructing veil of greed! (RUMI, *Mathnavi*, vol 2, story I)

> The intoxication of life and its pleasures and occupations veils the Truth from men's eyes . . . (RUMI, *Mathnavi*, vol 6, story III)

> (God) said to me, "Do you know how many veils I have veiled you with?" "No," I replied. He said, "With seventy

veils . . . " (IBN 'ARABI, *Contemplation of the Holy Mysteries,*
ISLÁMIC POET)

The most grievous of all veils is the veil of knowledge.
(BAHÁ'U'LLÁH quoting from a Hadith, *Kitáb-i-Íqán,*
187)

The unseen God is hidden from view and must be seen with spiritual
eyes.

Partial knowledge can become a barrier to growing in faith. When
a person thinks that he knows fully, he is no longer open to learning. This veil hinders one's spiritual progress and blocks the reception
of new divine truths. In fact, since God's knowledge is infinite, He
always has something to teach us. Therefore, no matter how much we
have learned about a topic, our task is to maintain an attitude of learning so that we keep open the door to further insights.

How can veils be removed?

In the symbolism of the Prayer, "fire" removes "veils." What is this
fire? A passion for truth, coupled with a humble acknowledgement
of how much we have to learn, facilitates the removal of obstacles
and consequently enhances our capacity to learn.

Due to the power of revelation to cut through veils, the Manifestations of God are said to have "eyes of fire." In explaining the
description of Christ in the New Testament Book of Revelation
1:14, Bahá'u'lláh comments:

"His (Christ's) eyes were as a flame of fire," He alludeth
but to the keenness of sight and acuteness of vision of the
Promised One, Who with His eyes burneth away every veil
and covering, maketh known the eternal mysteries . . . For,
indeed, what fire is fiercer than this flame that shineth in
the Sinai of His eyes, whereby He consumeth all that hath

veiled the peoples of the world? (Baháʼuʼlláh, *Gems of Divine Mysteries*, 54)

Impact of removing veils

By the fire of the Love of God the veil is burnt which separates us from the Heavenly Realities, and with clear vision we are enabled to struggle onward and upward, ever progressing in the paths of virtue and holiness, and becoming the means of light to the world. (ʼAbduʼl-Bahá, *Paris Talks*, 82)

A brief account of Baháʼuʼlláh's return for self-imposed exile in the mountains of Sulaymáníyyih illustrates the great impact that the Manifestation of God and His teachings have on the spiritual conduct and progress of the community of believers.

. . . fragmentary accounts of Him were circulated in all quarters and directions, to wit that a stranger, a Persian, had appeared in the district of Sulaymaniyyih . . . From the rumor thus heard it was known that that Person was none other than Baháʼuʼlláh. Several persons, therefore, hastened thither, and began to entreat and implore, and the urgent entreaty of all brought about His return.

. . . since the Báb was but beginning to lay the foundations when He was slain, therefore was this community ignorant concerning its proper conduct, action, behavior, and duty, their sole guiding principle being love for the Báb. This ignorance was the reason that in some parts disturbances occurred; for, experiencing violent molestation, they unclosed their hands in self-defense. But after His return Baháʼuʼlláh made such strenuous efforts in educating, teaching, training, regulating, and reconstructing this community that in a short while all these troubles and mischiefs were quenched, and the utmost tranquility and repose reigned in men's hearts; so that, according to what hath been heard, it became clear and obvious even to statesmen that the fundamental intentions and ideas of this sect were things spiritual, and such as are connected with pure hearts; that their true and essential principles were to reform the morals and beautify the conduct of the human race, and that with things material they had absolutely no concern. ('ABDU'L-BAHÁ, *A Traveller's Narrative*, 38)

... *shut me out from Thy beauty...*

In Sufi poetry, the person seeking intimacy with God is often compared to a lover seeking her or his beloved. In the eyes of a young couple, nothing is more beautiful than their adored one. Hearts melt with romance and the world takes on a special brightness. To share time together is the ultimate joy. By contrast, separation causes intense heartache. So it is in our relationship with God. Nothing is sweeter than time spent with our Creator in prayer and meditation.

> The voice of my beloved! Behold, he cometh leaping upon the mountains, skipping upon the hills . . . My beloved spoke, and said unto me, "Rise up, my love, my fair one, and come away. For, lo, the winter is past, the rain is over and gone. The flowers appear on the earth; the time of the singing of birds is come, and the voice of the turtle is heard in our land . . . Arise, my love, my fair one, and come away." (SONG OF SOLOMON 2:8–13, where the love of a young man and woman becomes a metaphor for the relationship between God and His people.)

> And one day he asked this witness in what her prayer consisted, and she replied: 'In considering the beauty of God and in rejoicing that He has such beauty.' And the Saint was so pleased with this that for some days he said the most sublime things concerning the beauty of God, at which all marveled. And thus, under the influence of this love, he composed five stanzas, beginning 'Beloved, let us sing, And in thy beauty see ourselves portray'd. (ST. JOHN OF THE CROSS, *Ascent of Mount Carmel*, CHRISTIAN MYSTIC)

> Because of his transcendence, God cannot be seen as He is, unless He himself opens up His mystery to man's immediate contemplation and gives him the capacity for it. The

Church calls this contemplation of God in his heavenly glory "the beatific vision." (CATHOLIC CATECHISM, 1028)

And when He purposed to manifest His beauty in the kingdom of names and to reveal His glory in the realm of attributes, He brought forth His Prophets from the invisible plane to the visible, that His name "the Manifest" might be distinguished from "the Hidden". . . (BAHÁ'U'LLÁH, *Gems of Divine Mysteries*, 32)

Should there be ignited in thy heart the burning brand of the love of God, thou wouldst seek neither rest nor composure, neither laughter nor repose, but wouldst hasten to scale the highest summits in the realms of divine nearness, sanctity, and beauty. (BAHÁ'U'LLÁH, *Gems of Divine Mysteries*, 13)

If the mystic knowers be of those who have reached to the beauty of the Beloved One, this station is the apex of consciousness and the secret of divine guidance. (BAHÁ'U'LLÁH, *The Four Valleys*, 56)

. . . a light that will lead me . . .

Light is, perhaps, one of the most universal symbols of knowledge. Our sense of vision is, for most of us, the primary way we learn about the physical world around us. When it comes to things that

cannot be seen with our physical eyes, light becomes a metaphor for comprehension. This metaphor has worked its way into popular culture in sayings, such as ". . . in the light of new evidence . . ." In ancient times, stars were used for navigation. When we walk, light allows us to know where we are going. As such, light serves as a guide to lead us in a desired direction. In spiritual matters, light refers to divine knowledge as in understanding the value of virtue and compliance with God's law.

> Thy word is a lamp unto my feet, and a light unto my path. (PSALMS 119:105, Hebrew scripture)

> God is the light of the heavens and the earth; His light is as a niche in which is a lamp, and the lamp is in a glass, the glass is as though it were a glittering star; it is lit from a blessed tree, an olive neither of the east nor of the west, the oil of which would well-nigh give light though no fire touched it,-light upon light!-God guides to His light whom He pleases. (QUR'ÁN 24:35, ISLÁMIC SCRIPTURE)

> The more the world of humanity develops, the more the effulgences or emanations of Divinity will become revealed, just as the stone, when it becomes polished and pure as a mirror, will reflect in fuller degree the glory and splendor of the sun. The mission of the Prophets, the revelation of the Holy Books, the manifestation of the heavenly Teachers and the purpose of divine philosophy all center in the training of the human realities so that they may become clear and pure as mirrors and reflect the light and love of the Sun of Reality. ('ABDU'L- BAHÁ, *The Promulgation of Universal Peace,* 59)

> That which is truly spiritual must light the path to God, and must result in deeds. (*'Abdu'l-Bahá in London,* 107)

. . . *unto the Ocean of Thy presence*

A Visualization Meditation—The Ocean of God's Presence:

Let us become quiet and still. Using imagination alone, begin drawing a mental picture of your prayer goal, the conclusion of your arduous trek finally arriving at the Ocean of God's Presence.

You are standing at the edge of the water on a pre-dawn beach. Surrounded by dark sky and dark waters stretching endlessly to the edge of sight. Gentle waves lap at your toes. Unhurriedly, a faint glow creeps over the eastern horizon. Daybreak approaches. Silhouettes of dark clouds begin to immerge against the deep gray rim of the sky that blends to indigo, then pink, then crimson.

However, only the sky's colors can be seen. The sun's disk remains veiled by the clouds now billowing white. Millions of droplets of water, each grab and scatter a photon bundle, veil the sun, depriving us of a direct view of the ascending sun. As the day's heat increases, the clouds thin and burn away. The sun's light penetrates all veils and appears as a burnished ball; its rays shimmering in exquisite beauty. Even the early dawning light is too bright for our frail eyes to safely gaze upon. At midday, the sun's light will be many times more intense.

In this way, the physical reality of the sun becomes a metaphor for God's inaccessibility. We are only able to see glimpses of the All-Glorious. Yet this token awareness is sufficient to stir the heart and create a passion for spiritual discovery. The quest is worth our every effort and exertion.

The ocean as a place of divine encounter

> Thou art He, O my God, Who hath unlocked the gate of heaven with the key of Thy Name . . . and hast summoned all mankind to the ocean of Thy presence. They rose up and rushed forth to attain the Ocean of Thy meeting, and the Horizon of Thy beauty . . . They were so inebriated

with the wine of their reunion with Thee, that they rid themselves of all attachment to whatever they themselves and others possessed. (BAHÁ'U'LLÁH, *Prayers and Meditations*, 267)

No man shall attain the shores of the ocean of true understanding except he be detached from all that is in heaven and on earth. Sanctify your souls, O ye peoples of the world, that haply ye may attain that station which God hath destined for you. (BAHÁ'U'LLÁH, *Kitáb-i-Íqán*, 3)

Ocean of Light

The vastness of the Ocean is another fitting symbol of the boundless knowledge of God.

> They shall not hurt nor destroy in all my holy mountain: for the earth shall be full of the knowledge of the LORD, as the waters cover the sea. (ISAIAH 11:9, HEBREW SCRIPTURE)

As such, in the Bahá'í Writings, we often find light imagery and ocean imagery in parallel.

> Make them signs of guidance, standards of Thine immortal kingdom, waves of the sea of Thy mercy, mirrors of the light of Thy majesty. ('ABDU'L-BAHÁ, *Bahá'í Prayers, 111)*

> . . . enter the paradise of the spiritual Kingdom, diffuse the lights of the Sun of Truth, cause the waves of this Most Great Ocean to reach all human souls so that this world of earth may be transformed into the world of heaven . . . ('ABDU'L-BAHÁ, *The Promulgation of Universal Peace*, 461)

> His Great Revelation . . . which God hath ordained to be an ocean of light for the sincere among His servants . . . (*Tablets of Bahá'u'lláh*, 101)

SECTION 2

More Than Words

Accompanying the words of the Long Obligatory Prayer are various instructions. These include 1) ablutions (the rinsing of the hands and face), 2) facing the Qiblih (the resting place of Bahá'u'lláh) and 3) specific postures to accompany each of the fifteen paragraphs of the prayer.

Ablutions

> It hath been ordained that every believer in God,
> . . . shall, each day, having washed his hands and then
> his face, . . . Perform . . . ablutions for the Obliga-
> tory Prayer. (Bahá'u'lláh, *Kitáb-i-Aqdas* 26)

Value and meaning of washing prior to prayer

Although literal water is intended, the act of washing carries spiritual meaning, namely recognition of the need to cleanse ourselves from deviations from the will of God, either conscious or unconscious, of commission or omission.

The usage of water is a symbol with ancient history. Hindus wash in the Ganges River. Jews use a mikvah (bath of running water) for spiritual purification. Christian baptism represents conversion, a rebirth, a once for all cleansing from the sins of the past and the beginning of a new life in Christ.

Likewise, the Bahá'í Faith recognizes the spiritual value of washing as a symbol of detachment from the world and full devotion to our Creator.

Strengthen my hand, O my God, that it may take hold of Thy Book with such steadfastness that the hosts of the world shall have no power over it. (BAHÁ'U'LLÁH, *Prayers and Meditations by Bahá'u'lláh*, 314)

Substitute Verse

The commandment of God, in this case as in so many others, makes provision for extenuating cases.

Let him that findeth no water for ablution repeat five times the words "In the Name of God, the Most Pure, the Most Pure," and then proceed to his devotions. (BAHÁ'U'LLÁH, *Kitáb-i-Aqdas*, 23)

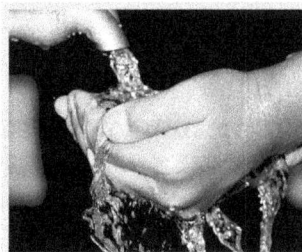

Facing the Qiblih

Bahá'u'lláh ordained that after His passing His burial place should become the Qiblih for the Bahá'í community, the Most Holy Tomb that is located at Bahjí, 'Akká in the Holy Land. With the simple act of turning to face the Spot of Adoration, we create an awareness within ourselves of entering sacred space.

Most Holy Tomb that is located at Bahjí, 'Akká in the Holy Land

'Abdu'l-Bahá describes that Spot as the "Luminous Shrine," "the place around which circumambulate the Concourse on High." In a letter written on his behalf, Shoghi Effendi uses a natural metaphor to explain the spiritual significance of turning towards the Qiblih:

> . . . just as the plant stretches out to the sunlight—from which it receives life and growth—so we turn our hearts to the Manifestation of God, Bahá'u'lláh, when we pray . . . we turn our faces . . . to where His dust lies on this earth as a symbol of the inner act. (Notes to the *Kitáb-i-Aqdas*, 170)

The direction one should face when praying will vary with one's location on earth. From North America, one generally faces eastward, but from places in central and southern Africa, one would fact northeast, from India, west, etc. Many use the web application found at Qiblih.com when traveling.

Facing the Qiblih only for obligatory prayer

Turning toward the Qiblih is a unique aspect of the Obligatory Prayers. No geographic direction is specified for other Bahá'í prayers.

> . . . for other prayers and devotions one may follow what the merciful Lord hath revealed in the Qur'án: "Whichever way ye turn, there is the face of God." (BAHÁ'U'LLÁH, *Kitáb-i-Aqdas*, 111, quoting Qur'án 2:115)

Why is the Qiblih specified for some prayers but not for others?

The two distinct practices, one for Obligatory Prayers and another for all other prayers, carry two significant lessons. In the first case, we learn of the indispensable role that the founding prophets play in our relationship with God, such that communication with our Creator is directed through them. In the second case, we learn that God is omnipresent. His presence surrounds us and He is approachable whichever way we face. These two great truths stand side-by-side.

What is the history of the direction of prayer in previous religions?

> That thine eyes may be open toward this house night and day, even toward the place of which thou hast said, My name shall be there: that thou mayest hearken unto the prayer which thy servant shall make toward this place. [Prayer of King Solomon at Dedication of Jerusalem Temple] (1 KINGS 8:27, Hebrew scripture)

> And Daniel . . . went into his house—now his windows were open in his upper chamber toward Jerusalem—and he kneeled upon his knees three times a day, and prayed, and gave thanks before his God . . . (DANIEL 6:11, Hebrew scripture)

> We prayed along with the Prophet facing Jerusalem for sixteen or seventeen months. Then Allah ordered him to turn his face towards the Qiblih (in Mecca) . . . (HADITH, *Bukhari,* vol 6, Islámic tradition)

What is the inner significance of the change in the Qiblih?

From Bahá'u'lláh, we learn the severity of the reaction of Muhammad's followers to the changing of the Qiblih from Jerusalem to Mecca.

> On a subsequent day, when the Prophet, together with His companions, was offering the noontide prayer, and had already performed two of the prescribed Rik'ats, the Voice of Gabriel was heard again: "Turn Thou Thy face towards the sacred Mosque." In the midst of that same prayer, Muhammad suddenly turned His face away from Jerusalem and faced the Ka'bih (in Mecca). Whereupon, a profound dismay seized suddenly the companions of

Jerusalem, the Qiblih from Solomon until Muhammad.

the Prophet. Their faith was shaken severely. So great was their alarm, that many of them, discontinuing their prayer, apostatized their faith. Verily, God caused not this turmoil but to test and prove His servants. (BAHÁ'U'LLÁH, *Kitáb-i-Íqán*, 49)

Why did changing this ancient tradition cause such a vehement reaction? And what spiritual lessons can be drawn from this incident?

• God's law can change over time. Spiritual growth often involves giving up long-standing practices and trying new approaches. God's program for our spiritual education involves various lessons that progressively lead to spiritual advancement.

- Blind imitation and loyalty to the way we have always done things can be a hindrance to full devotion to our Creator.

- Changes can bring tests of faith.

Yea, such things as throw consternation into the hearts of all men come to pass only that each soul may be tested by the touchstone of God, that the true may be known and distinguished from the false . . . Were you to ponder, but for a while, these utterances in your heart, you would surely find the portals of understanding unlocked before your face, and would behold all knowledge and the mysteries thereof unveiled before your eyes. Such things take place only that the souls of men may develop and be delivered from the prison-cage of self and desire. (BAHÁ'U'LLÁH, *Kitáb-i-Íqán*, 51)

Question for contemplation:

What issues may cause similar tests of faith in our day or in our lives?

Prayer Postures

The fifteen paragraphs of the Long Obligatory prayer are each preceded by an instruction directing a specific prayer posture or action: standing, turning the head, raising hands, kneeling, bowing, bending down with hands on knees, or sitting. Three of the fifteen postures include reciting the Greatest Name, Alláh-u-Abhá and one involve reciting the verse "Greater is God than every Great One."

Only in one case is the spiritual meaning of the action specifically explained. Preceding the opening paragraph, the instruction is given: "gaze to the right and left as if awaiting the mercy of His Lord." The action is clearly symbolic as no one can physically experience an abstract attribute such as the mercy of God. The wording "as if" likewise points to a symbolic meaning indicating that the one who prays this prayer waits in expectation of a spiritual encounter.

How does one experience "the mercy of His Lord?" There are, of course, many ways that we benefit from God's kindnesses. In this context, the prayer's purpose is to approach God's presence. His "mercy" then would be His willingness to receive us.

In other cases, the spiritual meaning of prayer postures, while not explicitly given, is fairly self-evident. Raising of the hand in supplication is an action of pleading. We are, in effect, beseeching "Please God, hear my prayer." When the instructions contain the words "in supplication" they are generally followed by a specific request, such as "Make of my prayer a fountain of living waters . . . "

Kneeling, bending and bowing down, especially with forehead to the ground are tokens of humility before the Sovereign of the

Universe, a physical symbol of our recognition of God's greatness much like bowing before a king.

The phrase "Greater is God than every great one!" also contains a valuable spiritual message. One might wonder, "Why such an obvious statement would be emphasized." Part of the answer may lie in the Bahá'í teachings against "joining partners" with God. Pure monotheism avoids confusing the station of the divine prophets with the Essence of God.

> Under no circumstances . . . can we, while repeating the prayers, insert the name Bahá'u'lláh where the word 'God' is used. This would be tantamount to blasphemy. (SHOGHI EFFENDI, *Directives from the Guardian*, 59)

Below is a complete list of the fifteen movements accompanying the Long Obligatory Prayer.

1. Whoso wisheth to recite this prayer, let him stand up and turn unto God, and, as he standeth in his place, let him gaze to the right and to the left, as if awaiting the mercy of his Lord, the Most Merciful, the Compassionate. Then let him say:
2. Let him then raise his hands in supplication toward God—blessed and exalted be He—and say:
3. Let him then kneel, and bowing his forehead to the ground, let him say:
4. Let him then stand and say:
5. Let him again raise his hands in supplication, and say:
6. Let him then raise his hands, and repeat three time the Greatest Name. Let him then bend down with hands resting on the knees before God—blessed and exalted be He—and say:
7. Let him then stand and raise his hands twice in supplication, and say:

8. Let him then raise his hands thrice, and say:
9. Let him then kneel and, bowing his forehead to the ground, say:
10. Let him then seat himself and say:
11. Let him then stand erect and say:
12. Let him then repeat the Greatest Name thrice, and bend down with hands resting on the knees, and say:
13. Let him then rise and say:
14. Let him then repeat the Greatest Name thrice, and kneel with his forehead to the ground, and say:
15. Let him then raise his head, and seat himself, and say:

Open questions

How exactly are these prayer postures to be performed? For example, how can someone bow with head to the ground while holding a prayer book? When asked to raise hands, how high should they be lifted? Should one's palms be turned toward the face? (This instruction is found in the Medium Obligatory Prayer, but not specified for the Long Obligatory Prayer.)

Since we have no authoritative guidance on these and other similar points, each of us is left to our own discretion on how we implement the instructions. Some believers will likely feel most comfortable following practices that are similar to those in Islamic societies or their own surrounding religious cultures, but in the absense of authoritative scriptural instruction, there is a need for caution that no one impose a private interpretation on others.

SECTION 3

O Thou the Desire of the World

The remainder of this commentary covers only selected phrases of the Prayer which are highlighted by bold and underline on the opening page of each section.

Let him then raise his hands in supplication toward God—blessed and exalted be He— and say:

O Thou the Desire of the world and the Beloved of the nations! Thou seest me turning toward Thee, and rid of all attachment to anyone save Thee, and clinging to Thy cord, through whose movement the whole creation hath been stirred up. I am Thy servant, O my Lord, and the son of Thy servant . . . . I implore Thee by the Ocean of Thy mercy and the Daystar of Thy grace to do with Thy servant as Thou willest and pleasest . . . . Whatsoever is revealed by Thee is the desire of my heart and the beloved of my soul . . . . By Thy Most Great Name, O Thou Lord of all nations! I have desired only what Thou didst desire, and love only what Thou dost love.

Let him then kneel, and bowing his forehead to the ground, let him say:

Exalted art Thou above the description of anyone save Thyself, and the comprehension of aught else except Thee.

Let him then stand and say:

Make my prayer, O my Lord, a fountain of living waters whereby I may live as long as Thy sovereignty endureth, and may make mention of Thee in every world of Thy worlds.

Let him again raise his hands in supplication, and say:

O Thou in separation from Whom hearts and souls have melted, and by the fire of Whose love the whole world hath been set aflame! Thou seest, O my Lord, this stranger hastening to his most exalted home beneath the canopy of Thy majesty and within the precincts of Thy mercy; and this transgressor seeking the ocean of Thy forgiveness; and this lowly one the court of Thy glory; and this poor creature the orient of Thy wealth . . . .

. . . Desire of the world . . .

Calling God "the Desire of the world" points to the natural human longing to know and love our Creator. Having been made in the image and likeness of God, humans all have spiritual needs. If unfulfilled, we are left hungry.

There is a God shaped vacuum in the heart of every man .
. . This he tries in vain to fill with everything around him,
seeking in things that are not there the help he cannot find
in those that are, though none can help, since this infinite
abyss can be filled only with an infinite and immutable
object; in other words by God himself. (BLAISE PASCAL,
Pensees 10.148, Christian philosopher)

Longing for communion with something greater than ourselves

Part of humanity's common spiritual heritage is a universal sense of
reverence, a feeling that there is something greater than ourselves to
which we strive to understand.

It is not we alone who pray; All things pray.
All things pour forth their souls.
The heavens pray; the earth prays, every creature and every
   living thing prays. In all life, there is longing.
Creation itself is but a longing, a prayer to the Almighty.
What are the clouds, the rising and the setting of the sun,
The soft radiance of the moon, and the gentleness of the
   night?
What are the flashes of the human mind and the storms of
   the human heart? They are all prayers—the outpouring
   of the boundless longing for God.
(MISHKAN T'FILAH, 287, *Reform Jewish Prayer Book*)

Let the sea resound and everything in it.

Let the rivers clap their hands,
Let the mountains sings together for joy;
Let them sing before the LORD, for He comes . . .
(PSALMS 98:7–9, Hebrew scripture)

Tvamekam varenyam. O Thou, my one desire . . .
(TRADITIONAL HINDU CHANT)

A thousand times, O prince incomparable,
Has my reason taken flight in desire to see thee,
And to hear thee and to listen to thy words,
And to behold thy life-giving smiles?
(RUMI, *Mathnavi*, Vol. 3, Story XVII, Islámic poet)

At the dawn of every day he should commune with God,
and with all his soul persevere in the quest of his Beloved.
He should consume every wayward thought with the flame
of His loving mention, and, with the swiftness of lightning,
pass by all else save Him. (BAHÁ'U'LLÁH, *Kitáb-i-Íqán*, 193)

Our natural desire to live a full, rich life, to be protected from intentionally or unintentionally hurting ourselves or others, our desire
for happiness and peace are dependent on the teachings of God. As
Creator, He best knows how the material universe works and can
provide the best set of instructions on how to live.

To him who holds in his hands the Great Image (of the
invisible Tao), the whole world repairs. Men resort to him,
and receive no hurt, but (find) rest, peace, and the feeling
of ease. (TAO TE CHING, Chinese scripture)

I am the Lord your God, who teaches you what is best for
you, who directs you in the way you should go. If only you
had paid attention to my commands, your peace would
have been like a river, your well-being like the waves of the
sea. (ISAIAH 48:17–18, Hebrew scripture)

Ye were created to show love one to another and not per-
versity and rancour. Take pride not in love for yourselves
but in love for your fellow-creatures. Glory not in love for

your country, but in love for all mankind. Let your eye be chaste, your hand faithful, your tongue truthful and your heart enlightened. (BAHÁ'U'LLÁH, *Tablets of Bahá'u'lláh*, 138)

The benefits of the advent and revelation of God accrue not only to the individual by instilling virtuous conduct, but also to society as a whole.

They whom God hath endued with insight will readily recognize that the precepts laid down by God constitute the highest means for the maintenance of order in the world and the security of its peoples.(BAHÁ'U'LLÁH, *Kitáb-i-Aqdas*, 19)

In the divine Holy Books, there are unmistakable prophecies giving the glad tidings of a certain day in which a promised one would appear to establish peace and reconcile long standing disputes.

He will teach us his ways, so that we may walk in his paths . . .

He will judge between the nations and will settle disputes for many peoples.

They will beat their swords into plowshares and their spears into pruning hooks. Nation will not take up sword against nation, nor will they train for war anymore.

Come, descendants of Jacob, let us walk in the light of the Lord. (ISAIAH 2:3–5, Hebrew scripture)

Among the various nations and peoples of the world no enmity or hatred should remain. All hearts were to be connected one with another. These things are recorded in the Torah, or Old Testament, in the Gospel, the Qur'án, the Zend-Avesta, the books of Buddha and the book of Confucius. In brief, all the Holy Books contain these glad tidings. ('ABDU'L-BAHÁ, *The Promulgation of Universal Peace*, 220)

... rid of all attachment to anyone save Thee ...

What is the significance of detachment?

A vital element of communion with God is the spiritual orientation of our souls. Our jobs, our friends, our reputation, our possessions, our social status, our money, even our health are put in secondary positions. The more we "rid ourselves of all attachment to anyone save God," the more we set spiritual things as the highest priority in our lives.

> But, O my brother, when a true seeker determineth to take the step of search in the path leading to the knowledge of the Ancient of Days . . . That seeker must at all times put his trust in God, must . . . detach himself from the world of dust, and cleave unto Him Who is the Lord of Lords. (BAHÁ'U'LLÁH, *Kitáb-i-Íqán*, 191)

> A wise man, abandoning the principle of darkness, should cultivate what is pure . . . Those whose minds are thoroughly practiced in the factors of enlightenment, who find delight in freedom from attachment in the renunciation of clinging, free from the inflow of thoughts, they are like shining lights, having reached final liberation in the world. (BUDDHA, *Dhammapada*, The Wise Man, Sayings of the Buddha)

Again, the kingdom of heaven is like unto a merchant man, seeking goodly pearls: Who, when he had found one pearl of great value, went and sold all that he had, and bought it. (MATTHEW 13:45–46, Christian scripture)

The symbolism of the lotus

In Hinduism, the lotus blossom is a sacred symbol of detachment. Even though the lotus has its roots in the mud of the pond from which it grows and obtains nutrients, it is ever unsullied as it floats on the water above the pond. Any drop of water that touches the lotus immediately slides off. Thus, mud and rain do it no harm. Even the trampling foot of an elephant is said to be incapable of crushing its beautiful form. The blossom bobs under the water and re-emerges with perfect shape, unbent, unmarked, for all practical purposes, untouched. The lotus is flawless, ever pure and detached from the world.

Visualize, now, the mud out of which the lotus grows, as it lifts itself high into the air to absorb the sunlight. The lotus looks upward, away from the mud of its origins. Yet it cannot deny those origins, lest it die. Think of it as sustained by them—turned away not in contempt, but gratefully, in its aspiration toward higher realities.

Do not mentally reject what you've been in the past. See God's presence there also, in the mud of your human origins. See God rising through long, arduous effort to reclaim Himself in the Great Self; God in the sunlight; God as the eternally shining, ever-blissful Sun." (SWAMI KRIYANANDA *Awaken to Superconsciousness*, Hindu commentary)

One who performs his duty without attachment . . . is as the lotus leaf, untouched by mud and water. (BHAGAVAD GITA 5:10, Hindu scripture)

The Bahá'í House of Worship in New Delhi,
India, is shaped as a lotus blossom, an
ancient Hindu symbol of detachment.

... *clinging to Thy cord* ...

What does "cord" symbolize?

Ancient robes were worn draped over the body, secured with a belt-like cord, often with one or both ends of the cord hanging down to the hem of the robe. The ill or the lame one, sitting on the ground, would reach up, grabbing the hem or the cord, seeking the attention of the wearer in order to plead for aid or ask to come under His protection.

"Clinging to the cord" thus becomes a symbol of willingness to give up the self-absorbed inadequacies of one's former life and to begin a new way of life in the household of a protective master. Implied is a devotion to the master, an expectation of obedience with a commitment to live by the rules of the household.

Clinging to God's cord signifies grasping and holding on, a devotion to God's Cause and Service.

> And hold ye fast by the cord of God, all of you, and break not loose from it; and remember God's goodness towards you, how that when ye were enemies, He united your hearts, and by his favour ye became brethren. (Quran 3:98, Islámic scripture)

> God says in the Qur'án: "Take ye hold of the Cord of God, all of you, and become ye not disunited." ('ABDU'L-BAHÁ, *Tablets of the Divine Plan*, 101)

> The betterment of the world hath been the sole aim of this Wronged One . . . Whilst afflicted with trials, He held fast unto the cord of patience and fortitude . . . (BAHÁ'U'LLÁH, *Epistle to the Son of the Wolf*, 36–37)

"Clinging to the skirt" or "hem of God's robe" is another figure of speech that sometimes carries a similar meaning. Putting oneself under the shadow of another's robe indicated a request for that person's protection.

> Yea, many peoples and mighty nations shall come to seek the LORD of hosts in Jerusalem . . .
>
> In those days it shall come to pass, that ten men shall take hold, out of all the languages of the nations, shall even take hold of the skirt of him that is a Jew, saying: We will go with you, for we have heard that God is with you.' (ZECHARIAH 8:23, Hebrew scripture)

> Cling thou to the hem of the Robe of God, and take thou firm hold on His Cord. (BAHÁ'U'LLÁH, *Gleanings from the Writings of Bahá'u'lláh*, 307)

> I am Thy servant who hath laid hold on the cord of Thy tender mercies, and clung to the hem of Thy bounteousness. (BAHÁ'U'LLÁH, *Prayers and Meditations by Bahá'u'lláh*, 224)

. . . through whose movement the whole creation hath been stirred up

God's Cord Stirs Creation

Here, the movement of God's cord is shown to have a universal impact. The Messengers of God come into the world to transform it, to bring new knowledge and new insights, to provide guidance on the issues of the day and to contribute to the advancement of civilization. Fresh breezes blow. New light shines. Events unfold so as to produce historical turning points. None are immune to its force.

The Day of the Lord—A Day of Visitation

A prominent example of the Creator of the world as playing a role in the flow of history can be seen in the Biblical narrative of the Israelite's exodus from Egypt. There, God acted on behalf of an entire nation.

> And God said moreover unto Moses . . . Go, and gather the elders of Israel together, and say unto them, The LORD God of your fathers, the God of Abraham, of Isaac, and of Jacob, appeared unto me, saying, I have surely visited you, and seen that which is done to you in Egypt: And I have said, I will bring you up out of the affliction of Egypt unto the land of the Canaanites, and the Hittites, and the Amorites, and the Perizzites, and the Hivites, and the Jebusites, unto a land flowing with milk and honey. (EXODUS 3:15–17. Hebrew scripture)

The recognition that God acts for the advancement of peoples and human society as a whole, changes our perception of the nature of

God. He is more than Creator of the World who, after bringing the universe into existence, turns passive and is no longer involved with His creation. He is not a passive god who stands at a distance. Rather, God enters history to mold humanity and advance civilization. For example, the advent of Moses, as a Manifestation of God, resulted in the liberation of the Israelites from Egyptian bondage, and lead to the establishment of a prototype Kingdom of God under King David and King Solomon.

Impact of New Revelation upon humanity

The image of God's cord stirring creation implies movement, a change from former conditions. As the old world order fades, new religious laws and institutions are established. Many people find these changes unsettling and choose to resist. The resulting turmoil is an intrinsic part of the process of advancement. Various metaphors are used in sacred writings to describe this time of trouble. Society is compared to a house whose foundations are shaken, to seemingly permanent and immovable mountains being removed, to the sky being rolled up and replaced.

> No sooner had that Revelation been unveiled to men's eyes than the signs of universal discord appeared among the peoples of the world, and commotion seized the dwellers of earth and heaven, and the foundations of all things were shaken. (BAHÁ'U'LLÁH, *Prayers and Meditations by Bahá'u'lláh*, 295)

> The earth hath been shaken, and the mountains have passed away, and the angels have appeared, rank on rank, before Us. Most of the people are bewildered in their drunkenness and wear on their faces the evidences of anger. (*The Proclamation of Bahá'u'lláh*, 100)

> And all the host of heaven shall be dissolved, and the heavens shall be rolled together as a scroll: and all their host shall fall down . . . (ISAIAH 34:4, Hebrew scripture)

> We will have rolled up the world and all that is therein, and spread out a new order in its stead. (BAHÁ'U'LLÁH, *Gleanings from the Writings of Bahá'u'lláh*, 313)

Being "stirred" causes many to draw closer to God

> Yet once, it is a little while, and I will shake the heavens, and the earth, and the sea, and the dry land; And I will shake all nations, and the desire of all nations shall come (to worship their LORD): and I will fill this house with glory, saith the LORD of hosts. (HAGGAI 2:6–7, Hebrew scripture)

> I bear witness that in His person solidity and fluidity have been joined and combined . . . throughout the domains of Thy Revelation and creation, the souls of Thy servants were stirred up in their longing for Thy Kingdom . . . (BAHÁ'U'LLÁH, *Prayers and Meditations by Bahá'u'lláh*, 48)

The cord of God is in motion. The stirring shows that the cord signifies more than the bond between the Divine Sovereign and subject. The cord's movement fits nicely with the image of the cord as a waistband around the Robe of God as though the cord were hanging down from Heaven stirring creation as God walks the earth.

> Cling thou to the hem of the Robe of God, and take thou firm hold on His Cord, a Cord which none can sever. (BAHÁ'U'LLÁH, *Gleanings from the Writings of Bahá'u'lláh*, 307)

I am Thy servant . . . and the son of Thy servant.

Who are servants of God?

One of the special features of the Bahá'í Revelation is its perspective on unity. All are seen as servants of God, regardless of their beliefs and conduct. Since all are God's children, made in His image, all serve a purpose in the divine scheme. This aspect of servitude is present whether a person makes a conscious decision to serve God or is unaware of God's purposes and guidance.

> All are His servants and all abide by His bidding. (THE BÁB, *Selections from the Writings of the Báb*, 215)

> O Thou kind Lord! Thou hast created all humanity from the same stock. Thou hast decreed that all shall belong to the same household. In Thy Holy Presence they are all Thy servants . . . ('ABDU'L-BAHÁ, *The Promulgation of Universal Peace*, 99)

Is it possible to be a servant of God without knowing it?

> To God prostrates everyone in the heavens and the earth, willingly or unwillingly, and so do their shadows in the mornings and the evenings. (QUR'ÁN 13:15, Islámic scripture)

> Verily, We behold all created things moved to bear witness unto Us. Some know Us and bear witness, while the majority bear witness, yet know Us not. (BAHÁ'U'LLÁH, *Tablets of Bahá'u'lláh*, 14)

In what sense can all be called God's servants?

> But in every great house there are not only vessels of gold
> and of silver, but also of wood and of earth; and some
> for honorable use and some to dishonorable use. If a man
> therefore purge himself from (what is unclean), he shall
> be a vessel of honor, sanctified, and suitable for the mas-
> ter's use, and prepared unto every good work. (2 TIMOTHY
> 2:20–22, Christian scripture)

> It is a self-evident truth that all humanity is the creation of
> God. All are His servants and under His protection. All are
> recipients of His bestowals. God is kind to all His servants.
> At most it is this: that some are ignorant; they must be
> educated . . . Some are immature as children; they must be
> aided and assisted in order that they may become mature.
> Some are sick and ailing; they must be healed. ('ABDU'L-
> BAHÁ, *The Promulgation of Universal Peace*, 39)

The wicked are called "God's servants."

It is noteworthy that Bahá'u'lláh called those who persecuted and
opposed Him "servants" of God. The inclusion of the ungodly as
servants of God emphasizes His Sovereignty over all. It also represents a paradigm shift from a perspective that divides humanity into
two distinct categories, the faithful and unfaithful, to a perspective
that emphasizes the unity of humanity as more fundamental than
any such distinction. All are the leaves of one tree.

> O God of the world and Lord of the nations! Thou behold-
> est our state and the things which have befallen us by
> reason of the cruelty of Thy servants. (BAHÁ'U'LLÁH, *Epistle
> to the Son of the Wolf*, 127)

Finally I fell a captive into the hands of the wayward among Thy servants. (BAHÁ'U'LLÁH, *Prayers and Meditations by Bahá'u'lláh*, 21)

What purpose do opposers of God serve?

God being All-Good, He would never allow trouble or pain unless it produced a greater good. Often hardship helps to clarify priorities and strengthen faith.

> Moreover, the more closely you observe the denials of those who have opposed the Manifestations of the divine attributes, the firmer will be your faith in the Cause of God. (BAHÁ'U'LLÁH, *Kitáb-i-Íqán*, 6)

> Does the soul progress more through sorrow or through the joy in this world?' . . . 'The mind and spirit of man advance when he is tried by suffering. The more the ground is ploughed the better the seed will grow . . . suffering and tribulation free man from the petty affairs of this worldly life until he arrives at a state of complete detachment. His attitude in this world will be that of divine happiness. Look back to the times past and you will find that the greatest men have suffered most. ('ABDU'L-BAHÁ, *Paris Talks*, 178)

> Moses and Pharaoh, alike doers of God's will,
> As Light and Darkness, Poison and Antidote.
> Verily, both Moses and Pharaoh walked in the appointed
>   way,
> Though seemingly the one did so, and the other not.
> By day Moses wept before God,
> At midnight Pharaoh lifted up his cry,
> Saying, "What a yoke is this upon my neck,
> O God! Were it not for this yoke, I would boast,

Yet Thou hast made Moses' face bright as the moon,
And hast made the moon of my face utter darkness . . .
(Yet) Moses and I are Thy nurslings both alike, ..."
(RUMI, *Mathnavi*, Vol. 1, Story IX, Islámic poetry)

Past revelation has not recognized unbelievers as servants of God

From one perspective, only those who do God's Will and by abide His law may be thought of as true, faithful servants of God. Past revelation has emphasized the distinction between those who live a godly life and those who do not.

> Then shall ye return, and discern between the righteous and the wicked, between him that serveth God and him that serveth him not. (MALACHI 3:18, Hebrew scripture)

> Again, the kingdom of heaven is like unto a net, that was cast into the sea, and gathered of every kind: Which, when it was full, they drew to shore, and sat down, and gathered the good into vessels, but cast the bad away. So shall it be at the end of the world: the angels shall come forth, and sever the wicked from among the just . . . , (MATTHEW 13:47–49, Christian scripture)

This same distinction, between the righteous and the wicked, is found in the Bahá'í Writings. Confusion is especially troubling when some individuals claim to be doing God's will, but in reality are not. Great injustice can result when harmful deeds are performed in God's name.

> Contemplate first the prejudice of religion: consider the nations of so-called religious people; if they were truly worshippers of God they would obey His law which for-

bids them to kill one another. If priests of religion really adored the God of love and served the Divine Light, they would teach their people to keep the chief Commandment, 'To be in love and charity with all men'. But we find the contrary, for it is often the priests who encourage nations to fight. Religious hatred is ever the most cruel! ('ABDU'L-BAHÁ, *Paris Talks*, 146)

Who is the "son of Thy servant?"

This phrase demonstrates the importance of family ties in the Bahá'í Revelation. By identifying ourselves as, not only God's servants, but also the sons of His servants, we recognize the care and gifts bestowed upon us by our parents. For those Bahá'ís whose parents are not Bahá'í, but who embraced the Faith based on their own, the phrase, "I am . . . the son of Thy servant" might raise questions. In what way are my parents serving God? The fact that we are actively seeking to do God's will implies that our parents have given us training in godly qualities that have facilitated our recognition of Bahá'u'lláh.

In addition, there is a spiritual family bond expressed in the Bahá'í writings between children and their parents regardless of whether the parents recognize the station of Bahá'u'lláh or not.

> After the recognition of the oneness of the Lord, exalted be He, the most important of all duties is to have due regard for the rights of one's parents. This matter hath been mentioned in all the Books of God . . . . (BAHÁ'U'LLÁH, Quoted in *Family life, a compilation of the Universal House of Justice*, #4)

Seeing our parents as spiritual adversaries can only have a negative effect on our relationship with them and on our family life. On the other hand, praying for one's parents and the giving of charity in the names of parents are especially potent with beneficial results, not only in this world but also in the world to come.

> It is seemly that the servant should, after each prayer, supplicate God to bestow mercy and forgiveness upon his parents. Thereupon God's call will be raised: 'Thousand upon thousand of what thou hast asked for thy parents shall be thy recompense!' Blessed is he who remembereth his parents when communing with God. (THE BÁB, *Selections from the Writings of the Báb*, 94)

> One of the distinguishing characteristics of this most great Dispensation is that the kin of such as have recognized and embraced the truth of this Revelation . . . will, upon their death, if they are outwardly non-believers, be graciously invested with divine forgiveness and partake of the ocean of His Mercy. (BAHÁ'U'LLÁH, Quoted in *Family life, a compilation of the Universal House of Justice*, #6)

> . . . parents endure the greatest toil and trouble for their children . . . The children must therefore, in return for this pain and trouble, make charitable contributions and perform good works in their name, and implore pardon and forgiveness for their souls. ('ABDU'L-BAHÁ, *Some Answered Questions*, 62, 6)

. . . *Ocean of Thy mercy* . . .

This phrase, "Ocean of Thy Mercy" and the one that follows, "Day-star of Thy grace, are parallel invocations that call upon God to hear our prayer because of His kindly attributes.

Spiritual meanings of ocean

The physical oceans of the world are vast, apparently boundless expanses, stretching from horizon to horizon. As such, "ocean" is a fitting symbol for the enormity of divine knowledge, love, mercy and other attributes of the infinite God.

In the Bahá'í Writings we find a variety of expressions extolling the boundless virtues of God. The ocean metaphor is one usage that stresses the vastness of God's divine attributes. Reference is made to many such oceans including the ocean of knowledge, the ocean of wisdom, the ocean of unity, the ocean of His eternal justice, the ocean of boundless forgiveness, the ocean of science, the ocean of Divine Revelation, limitless oceans of meaning.

Mercy is an underserved kindness—sometimes the forgiveness of sin and pardon from punishment. According to His good pleasure, God, who is judge of all, does not necessarily repay to each what is due by pure justice, as in "an eye for an eye," but rather overlooks faults, heals wounds, and reconciles His creation to Himself despite sins and errors, either intentional and unintentional.

> I testify, O my God, that I have put away Thy commandments, and clung to the dictates of my passions, and have cast away the statutes of Thy Book, and seized the book of mine own desire. O misery, misery! As mine iniquities waxed greater and greater, Thy forbearance towards me augmented, and as the fire of my rebelliousness grew fiercer, the more did Thy forgiveness and Thy grace seek

to smother up its flame. (Baháʼuʼlláh, *Epistle to the Son of the Wolf*, 5)

Bismillah al-Rahman, al-Rahim; In the name of Allah, the Beneficent, the Merciful. (Qurʼán 1:1, Islámic scripture)

What ye give tongue to so foolishly
Is as the words of spoiled children to their father.
I knew of myself what ye thought,
But I desired that ye should speak it;
As this boasting of yours is very improper,
So shall my mercy be shown to prevail over my wrath .
. . : My mercy equals that of a hundred fathers and
mothers;
Every soul that is born is amazed thereat.
Their mercy is as the foam of the sea of my mercy; It is
mere foam of waves, but the sea abides ever!
(Rumi, *Masnavi,* Vol 1, Islámic poet)

The LORD, the LORD, God, merciful and gracious, long-suffering, and abundant in goodness and truth; keeping mercy unto the thousandth generation, forgiving iniquity and transgression and sin . . . (Exodus 34:6–7, Hebrew scripture)

God's mercy is also displayed in that He compassionately condescends to deal with us, lowly creatures of dust that we are. In His gift of life and a creation of a beautiful world for us to live in, in sending down revealed guidance and instruction, He has shown us great undeserved kindness, for we could never earn or merit His multitudinous blessings.

All creatures that exist are dependent upon the Divine Bounty. Divine Mercy gives life itself. As the light of the sun shines on the whole world, so the Mercy of the infinite God is shed on all creatures. ('Abdu'l-Bahá, *Paris Talks*, 25)

Thou art, in truth, He Whose mercy hath encompassed all the worlds . . . I bear witness that Thou hadst turned toward Thy servants ere they had turned toward Thee, and hadst remembered them ere they had remembered Thee. All grace is Thine, O Thou in Whose hand is the kingdom of Divine gifts . . . (Bahá'u'lláh, *Prayers and Meditations by Bahá'u'lláh*, 253)

Ye are the saplings which the hand of Loving-kindness hath planted in the soil of mercy, and which the showers of bounty have made to flourish. He hath protected you from the mighty winds of misbelief, and the tempestuous gales of impiety, and nurtured you with the hands of His loving providence. (Bahá'u'lláh, *Epistle to the Son of the Wolf*, 25)

Benefiting from the Ocean of His Mercy

The ocean of divine providence is surging, but we must be able to swim. The bestowals of the Almighty are descending from the heaven of grace, but capacity to receive them is essential . . . Therefore, we must endeavor night and day to purify the hearts from every dross, sanctify the souls from every restriction and become free from the discords of the human world. Then the divine bestowals will become evident in their fullness and glory. ('Abdu'l-Bahá, *The Promulgation of Universal Peace*, 196)

Why is man so hard of heart? It is because he does not yet know God . . . If only the laws and precepts of the prophets of God had been believed, understood and followed, wars would no longer darken the face of the earth. If man had even the rudiments of justice, such a state of things would be impossible. Therefore, I say unto you pray—pray and turn your faces to God, that He, in His infinite compassion and mercy, may help and succour these misguided ones. Pray that He will grant them spiritual understanding and teach them tolerance and mercy, that the eyes of their minds may be opened and that they may be endued with the gift of the spirit. Then would peace and love walk hand in hand through the lands, and these poor unhappy people might have rest. ('Abdu'l-Bahá, *Paris Talks*, 115–116)

. . . *Daystar of Thy grace* . . .

"Grace," a divine attribute closely related to "mercy," signifies the free and unmerited favor of God. It encompasses undeserved kindness, acts of generosity that the recipient has done nothing to deserve. God grants us existence and blesses us, not due to any merit on our part (What merit could we have before we existed?), but as a free, unearned gift. Grace!

> O SON OF MAN!
>
> Veiled in My immemorial being and in the ancient eternity of My essence, I knew My love for thee; therefore I created thee, have engraved on thee Mine image and revealed to thee My beauty. (BAHÁ'U'LLÁH, *Hidden Words*, Arabic #3)

"Daystar" has many related meanings. It often is used as a synonym for the sun. Its appearance at dawn marks the start of each day.

> Hast thou commanded the morning since thy days; and caused the dayspring to know his place . . . (JOB 38.12, Hebrew scripture)

When used to describe spiritual realities, the daystar represents Divinity. The term can be used of God Himself. The sun is an appropriate symbol for the Supreme One as the brightest of lights.

> For the LORD God is a sun . . . (PSALMS 84:11, Hebrew scripture)

> . . . the Sun, which is the Essence of the Divinity . . . ('ABDU'L-BAHÁ, *Some Answered Questions*, 27, 7)

> He Who is the Daystar of Truth . . . The One true God . .
> . (Bahá'u'lláh, *Epistle to the Son of the Wolf*, 14)

At other times, "Daystar" can refer to the Manifestations of God, Who are messengers bringing the light of Divine Revelation into the world.

> Each time the Daystar of Divine Revelation shed its radiance from the horizon of God's Will a great number of men denied Him . . . (Bahá'u'lláh, *Epistle to the Son of the Wolf*, 64)

In His discussion of the Christian concept of the Trinity, 'Abdu'l-Bahá elaborates on the nature of the relationship between God and the Manifestations as suns (equivalent to daystars).

> God is pure perfection . . . His manifestation, dawning, and effulgence are even as the appearance of the sun in a clear, bright, and polished mirror . . . Now, if we were to say that we have beheld the Sun in two mirrors—one Christ and the other the Holy Spirit—or, in other words, that we have seen three Suns—one in heaven and two upon the earth—we would be speaking the truth. And if we were to say that there is only one Sun, that it is absolute singleness, and that it has no peer or partner, we would again be speaking the truth. ('Abdu'l-Bahá, *Some Answered Questions*, 27, 4, and 6)

Whatsoever is revealed by Thee is the desire of my heart . . .

The desire to be completely in sync with God's will is an ideal, rather than our day to day reality. From practical experience, we know that we do not always feel the way we want to feel. We slip. We forget. We do things that we regret. At times, we may have desires to say or do things contrary to the will of God. Yet, the spiritual life entails a striving to rein in such feelings and consequently to forestall inappropriate actions that might result. We struggle to do what is right, to rid ourselves of wayward desires, to bring our hearts into closer conformity with the spirit of faith. None of us is perfect in this regard. Day by day we hope to improve, to polish godly virtues and cleanse the mirror of our hearts in order to better reflect the glory of God. Having desires in perfect harmony with God's will is not where we are, but where we hope to be headed.

In modern terms, a statement such as this one that states a virtuous goal, as if it were already accomplished fact, might be called an "affirmation." Uttering such ideals helps to refashion our patterns of thought and to create a new inner reality.

O SON OF GLORY!

Be swift in the path of holiness, and enter the heaven of communion with Me. Cleanse thy heart with the burnish of the spirit, and hasten to the court of the Most High. (BAHÁ'U'LLÁH, *The Persian Hidden Words*, 8)

Beware lest the desires of the flesh and of a corrupt inclination provoke divisions among you. Be ye as the fingers of one hand, the members of one body. (BAHÁ'U'LLÁH, *Kitáb-i-Aqdas*, 40)

O God, my God! My back is bowed by the burden of my sins, and my heedlessness hath destroyed me. Whenever I ponder my evil doings and Thy benevolence, my heart melteth within me, and my blood boileth in my veins. (Bahá'u'lláh, *Prayers and Meditations by Bahá'u'lláh*, 322, Long Obligatory Prayer)

For I have the desire to do what is good, but I cannot carry it out.

For I do not do the good I want to do, but the evil I do not want to do—this I keep on doing. (Romans 7:18b–19, Christian scripture)

I have desired only what Thou didst desire . . .

What are the benefits of harmonizing our desires with God's will for us?

God as our Creator knows us, inside and out, heart, soul and mind. He knows us better than we know ourselves. Knowing what will make us happy and contribute to our wellbeing, His command-ments are crafted to benefit us. Accordingly, abiding by His com-mands with a spirit of joy and heartfelt desire will always be for our good. Even when we do not fully understand the reasons for His commandments, they will always be in our own best interests.

> Men keep their possessions for their own enjoyment and do not share sufficiently with others the bounty received from God. Spring is thus changed into the winter of self-ishness and egotism. Jesus Christ said 'Ye must be born again' so that divine Life may spring anew within you. Be kind to all around and serve one another; love to be just and true in all your dealings; pray always and so live your life that sorrow cannot touch you. Look upon the people of your own race and those of other races as members of one organism; sons of the same Father; let it be known by your behaviour that you are indeed the people of God. Then wars and disputes shall cease and over the world will spread the Most Great Peace." (*'Abdu'l-Bahá in London*, 82)

> Lord, make me an instrument of your peace.
> Where there is hatred, let me sow love.
> Where there is injury, pardon.
> Where there is doubt, faith.
> Where there is despair, hope.

Where there is darkness, light.
Where there is sadness, joy.
O Divine Master,
Grant that I may not so much seek to be consoled, as to
    console;
To be understood, as to understand;
To be loved, as to love.
For it is in giving that we receive.
It is in pardoning that we are pardoned,
And it is in dying that we are born to Eternal Life.
Amen.
(PRAYER OF ST. FRANCIS, Christian tradition)

This is what the Lord says, your Redeemer, the Holy One
    of Israel:
"I am the Lord your God, who teaches you what is best for
    you,
Who directs you in the way you should go.
If only you had paid attention to my commands,
Your peace would have been like a river,
your well-being like the waves of the sea . . . "
(ISAIAH 48:17–18, Hebrew scripture)

... *above the description of anyone save Thyself* ...

The divine essence is unknowable. God is unlike anything that material beings are capable of experiencing. We are able to get a glimpse of His glory by looking at the enormity of Creation, or by seeing His attributes reflected in the vast visible universe, yet any measure of understanding we may gain falls far short of fully describing His infinite nature. Only God can adequately comprehend Himself.

Humanity's inability to grasp the Divine Nature is illustrated in the story of Moses receiving the Ten Commandments on Mount Sinai. Even though He was allowed to hear God's voice, Moses was told that his mortal frame could not survive direct encounter with God.

> Then Moses said (to God), "Now show me your glory."
>
> And the LORD said, "I will cause all my goodness to pass in front of you, and I will proclaim my name, the LORD, in your presence. I will have mercy on whom I will have mercy, and I will have compassion on whom I will have compassion. But," he said, "you cannot see my face, for no one may see me and live."
>
> Then the LORD said, "There is a place near me where you may stand on a rock. When my glory passes by, I will put you in a cleft in the rock and cover you with my hand until I have passed by. Then I will remove my hand and you will see my back; but my face must not be seen." (EXODUS 33;18–23, Hebrew scripture)

God's inexplicable nature

> ... the divine Being, is immensely exalted beyond every human attribute ... Far be it from His glory that human tongue should adequately recount His praise, or that

human heart comprehend His fathomless mystery. He is and hath ever been veiled in the ancient eternity of His Essence . . . (BAHÁ'U'LLÁH, *Kitáb-i-Íqán*, 98)

No vision can grasp Him, but His grasp is over all vision: He is above all comprehension, yet is acquainted with all things. (Qur'án 6:103, Islámic scripture)

O the depth of the riches both of the wisdom and knowledge of God! How unsearchable his judgments are, and past tracing out his ways are! (ROMANS 11:33, Christian scripture)

Lord of the Universe . . . Glory be to thee, the tranquil, the deeply hidden, the incomprehensible, the immeasurable, without beginning and without end. (UPANISHADS, Fifth Prapatraka, Hindu scripture)

He is Unfathomable, Incomprehensible, Exalted and High, Eternal and Imperishable; His worth cannot be appraised (SHRI GURU GRANTH SAHIB, Section 30 – Raag Saarang, Sikh scripture)

Make my prayer a
fountain of living water . . .

Water is an ancient symbol of life. Man and beast can survive only a few short days without an adequate supply of fresh drinking water. Flowing, "living" water thus makes a fitting symbol of spiritual sustenance, which is a requirement of spiritual life. When ʿAbduʾl-Bahá prays, "May they drink from the same fountain," He expresses a spirit of unity where all share in the same divine bounty of spiritual water.

Water that instills life

> I implore Thee, by this very word that hath shone forth above the horizon of Thy will, to enable me to drink deep of the living waters through which Thou hast vivified the hearts of Thy chosen ones and quickened the souls of them that love Thee . . . (BAHÁʾUʾLLÁH, *Prayers and Meditations by Baháʾuʾlláh*, 6)

> Through worship man becometh spiritual, his heart is attracted, and his soul and inner being attain such tenderness and exhilaration that the Obligatory Prayer instilleth new life in him. (ʿABDUʾL-BAHÁ, *The Importance of Obligatory Prayer and Fasting*, IX)

Jesus and the Samaritan woman at the well

> So He (Christ) came to a city of Samaria called Sychar, near the parcel of ground that Jacob gave to his son Joseph; and Jacob's well was there. So Jesus, being wearied from His journey, was sitting thus by the well. It was about the sixth hour.
>
> There came a woman of Samaria to draw water. Jesus said to her, "Give Me a drink." For His disciples had gone away into the city to buy food. Therefore the Samaritan

woman said to Him, "How is it that You, being a Jew, ask me for a drink since I am a Samaritan woman?" (For Jews have no dealings with Samaritans.) Jesus answered and said to her, "If you knew the gift of God, and who it is who says to you, 'Give Me a drink,' you would have asked Him, and He would have given you living water." She said to Him, "Sir, You have nothing to draw with and the well is deep; where then do You get that living water? You are not greater than our father Jacob, are You, who gave us the well, and drank of it himself and his sons and his cattle?" Jesus answered and said to her, "Everyone who drinks of this water will thirst again; but whoever drinks of the water that I will give him shall never thirst; but the water that I will give him will become in him a well of water springing up to eternal life."

The woman said to Him, "Sir, give me this water . . . (JOHN 4:5–15, Christian scripture)

. . . make mention of Thee in every world of Thy worlds . . .

Every world of Thy worlds

God's promise of everlasting life holds open possibilities for our souls to progressively advance through all eternity in an endless array of future "worlds of God." Prayer is the portal through which we begin our journey to eternity. What adventures may be in store for us, what eons lay ahead, what various forms of existence we may have the bounty to experience, an infinite number of doors stand ready to be opened and entered under the endless blessings and guidance of our loving Creator.

What are the worlds of God?

> Know thou of a truth that the **worlds of God are countless** in their number, and infinite in their range. None can reckon or comprehend them except God, the All-Knowing, the All-Wise. (BAHÁ'U'LLÁH, *Tablets of Bahá'u'lláh*, 187)

> I refer to the Titanic disaster, in which many of our fellow human beings were drowned, a number of beautiful souls passed beyond this earthly life . . . When I think of them, I am very sad indeed. But when I consider this calamity in another aspect, I am consoled by the realization that the worlds of God are infinite; that though they were deprived of this existence, they have other opportunities in the life beyond, even as Christ has said, "In my Father's house are many mansions." They were called away from the temporary and transferred to the eternal; they abandoned this material existence and entered the portals of the spiritual world. ('ABDU'L-BAHÁ, *Promulgation of Universal Peace*, 46)

The world beyond is as different from this world as this world is different from that of the child while still in the womb of its mother. When the soul attaineth the Presence of God, it will assume the form that best befitteth its immortality and is worthy of its celestial habitation. (Bahá'u'lláh, *Gleanings from the Writings of Bahá'u'lláh*, 156)

Eye hath not seen, nor ear heard, neither have entered into the heart of man, the things which God hath prepared for them that love him. (1 Corinthians 2:9, Christian scripture)

. . . hearts and souls have melted . . .

Literal hearts do no melt, but we have all experienced the sensation of being so emotionally overwhelmed that we feel weak and formless, perhaps even incapable of moving. Often this sense of our own weakness is a preparatory step, a softening, that readies us to change, to learn, to be reformed.

> Every heart will melt with fear and every hand go limp; every spirit will become faint . . . (Ezekiel 21:7, Hebrew scripture)

> . . . in their peril their courage melted away.
> They reeled and staggered like drunkards;
> They were at their wits' end.
> Then they cried out to the Lord in their trouble,
> And he brought them out of their distress . . .
> (Psalms 107:26–28, Hebrew scripture)

> The hearts of Thy chosen ones, O my Lord, have melted because of their separation from Thee . . . I implore Thee, O Thou Maker of the heavens . . . to send down upon Thy loved ones that which will draw them nearer unto Thee, and enable them to hearken unto Thine utterances. (Bahá'u'lláh, *Prayers and Meditations by Bahá'u'lláh*, 7)

> I extol Thy virtues through the tongue of those of Thy people that have recognized Thy oneness, that haply there may pour out from the sighs which they utter in their love and their yearning for Thee what will melt away all that may hinder Thy servants from setting their faces towards the heaven of Thy knowledge and the kingdom of Thy signs. (Bahá'u'lláh, *Prayers and Meditations by Bahá'u'lláh*, 281)

. . . *this stranger* . . .

In the Ancient Near East, the stranger held an exalted position. Hospitality to strangers, in contrast to favors shown to a friend, was a sign of justice.

> For the Lord your God is God of gods and Lord of lords, the great God, mighty and awesome, who is not partial . . . who loves the strangers, providing them food and clothing. You shall also love the stranger, for you were strangers in the land of Egypt. (Deuteronomy 10:17–19, Hebrew scripture)

The Bahá'í Writings likewise embrace the stranger. In fact, since all humanity is viewed as one human family, the distinction between friend and stranger fades.

> We do not consider anyone a stranger, for it is said by Bahá'u'lláh 'Ye are all the rays of one sun; the fruits of one tree; and the leaves of one branch.' We desire the true brotherhood of humanity. (*'Abdu'l-Bahá in London*, 80)

In the context of our spiritual quest, we become "this stranger," a traveler, a spiritual wayfarer in search of a "home" with God. Despite God's welcome of seekers, we may feel like strangers, venturing into unknown places, forsaking well-known environs, taking up new beliefs and unfamiliar practices. The seeker should always be assured of God's love and a warm welcome in the community of seekers.

O BEFRIENDED STRANGER!

The candle of thine heart is lighted by the hand of My power, quench it not with the contrary winds of self and passion. The healer of all thine ills is remembrance of Me, forget it not. Make My love thy treasure and cherish it even as thy very sight and life. (BAHÁ'U'LLÁH, *The Persian Hidden Words*, 32)

. . . (this stranger) hastening to his most exalted home beneath the canopy of Thy majesty . . .

Realization of our true home

This beautiful image helps us move our consciousness from the material to the spiritual realm. Rather than seeing ourselves at home in the physical place where we lay our heads each night, our perspective is transformed. We are aided to see our current existence as alien to our true selves and to identify our real "home" as an exalted heavenly abode near God.

> . . . haply the sore athirst in the wilds of remoteness may attain unto the ocean of the divine presence, and they that languish in the wastes of separation be led unto the home of eternal reunion. (BAHÁ'U'LLÁH, *Kitáb-i-Íqán*, 19)

> In His Mercy, God unites us with Himself . . . I have obtained my home in the True Mansion of His Presence . . . (SHRI GURU GRANTH SAHIB, Sikh scripture)

An array of symbols is used in the Bahá'í writings to describe the spiritual goal of attaining nearness to God. In this phrase, our goal is compared to a heavenly home. In other passages, we find imagery related to the City of God, the human heart, the Ocean of His Presence, the Beloved, etc.

Getting close to God can be compared to a spiritual journey, as vividly depicted in Bahá'u'lláh's mystical works, *Four Valleys* and *Seven Valleys*. In them, the worshipper is symbolized as a sojourner wandering the earth, traversing challenging mountains and valleys in his search for his true home.

The stages that mark the wayfarer's journey from the abode of dust to the heavenly homeland are said to be seven. Some have called these Seven Valleys, and others, Seven Cities. (Bahá'u'lláh, *The Seven Valleys*, 4)

Wherefore, O friend, give up thy self that thou mayest find the Peerless One, pass by this mortal earth that thou mayest seek a home in the nest of heaven. (Bahá'u'lláh, *The Seven Valleys*, 9)

In 'Abdu'l-Bahá discussion of a verse from the Gospel of John, he shows that heaven often refers to a spiritual condition, rather than a physical place.

. . . in John 3:13 it is stated: "And no man hath ascended up to heaven, but He that came down from heaven, even the Son of man which is in heaven." . . . Consider how it is said that the Son of man is in heaven, even though at that time Christ was dwelling upon the earth . . . It is therefore clear that the assertion that the Son of man came down from heaven has a mystical rather than a literal meaning, and is a spiritual rather than a material event. ('Abdu'l-Bahá, *Some Answered Questions*, 23, 3–4)

Presence with God not a place in space

God does not exist in a physical location as some have imagined— not hovering above the earth on a throne, nor up in the sky in a distant galaxy, nor hidden in a secret spot on earth, nor residing in a sacred temple. God is outside of time and space. Therefore it is impossible to reach Him in any material sense. Rather the goal to achieve nearness to God is the quest for an internal spiritual condition, an elevated spiritual experience while physically present in this world. His Throne is a symbol of His majestic sovereignty.

. . . the one true God, alone and single, is established upon His Throne, a Throne which is beyond the reaches of time and space . . . (Bahá'u'lláh, *The Summons of the Lord of Hosts*, 110)

God's many mansions

Elaborating on the image of a home with the Lord, the sacred scriptures speak of God's heavenly mansions as places of residence for God's faithful servants in the next world.

> In my Father's house are many mansions: if it were not so, I would have told you. I go to prepare a place for you. And if I go and prepare a place for you, I will come again, and receive you unto myself; that where I am, there ye may be also. (John 14:2–3, Christian scripture)

> As to the worlds whereunto Christ referred-unto whom be great glory-(the many mansions)," writes 'Abdu'l-Bahá "they are spiritual, divine, heavenly, single, unlocated . . . " (*Star of the West*, XIV:2, 35)

Canopy of Thy Majesty

> . . . that I may dwell within the tabernacle of Thy majesty and beneath the canopy of Thy favour. (Bahá'u'lláh, *The Summons of the Lord of Hosts*, 125)

> But when He (Christ) declared that He had come from Heaven, it is clear that He did not mean the blue firmament but that He spoke of the Heaven of the Kingdom of God, and that from this Heaven He descended upon the clouds. ('Abdu'l-Bahá, *Paris Talks*, 44)

. . . orient of Thy wealth . . .

The fabled east has long been viewed as a source of wealth. Europeans and Middle Easterners long sought after Indian spices. Marco Polo's expedition to China brought Europe such innovations as Chinese silk, pearls, fireworks, gunpowder, printing, pasta and a rich artistic heritage.

As early as the second century CE, caravan routes overland from Europe to India and China provided the means to bring wealth of the East westward. Colonial powers in the 16th and 17th centuries established overseas shipping trade routes to bring the silk, spices and other commodities from Asia to the west. Wealth has long been associated with the orient.

What kind of wealth does the spiritual sojourner seek?

Material wealth can be a divine blessing when used to help the poor, to further the Cause of God or for the betterment of the world. However, the sacred scriptures concentrate on spiritual riches, using material wealth as a metaphor for having an abundance of divine knowledge and virtues

> . . . everyone who thirsts, come to the waters, and he that has no money; come buy, and eat; yes, come, buy wine and milk without money and without price. Why do you pay for that which is not true bread or labor for that which gives only temporary satisfaction? Listen diligently to me, and eat that which is good, and let your soul delight in fatness Incline your ear, and come to me: hear, and your soul shall live . . . (ISAIAH 55:1–3, Hebrew scripture)

> Then it is clear that the honour and exaltation of man cannot reside solely in material delights and earthly benefits. This material felicity is wholly secondary, while the

exaltation of man resides primarily in such virtues and attainments as are the adornments of the human reality. These consist in divine blessings, heavenly bounties . . . They consist in justice and equity, truthfulness and benevolence, inner courage and innate humanity, safeguarding the rights of others . . . They consist in rectitude of conduct under all circumstances, love of truth under all conditions . . . This is the felicity of the human world! ('ABDU'L-BAHÁ, *Some Answered Questions*, 15, 7)

SECTION 4

How My Spirit
Hath Been Stirred Up

Let him then raise his hands, and repeat three times the Greatest Name. Let him then bend down with hands resting on the knees before God—blessed and exalted be He—and say:

Thou seest, O my God, how my spirit hath been stirred up within my limbs and members, in its longing to worship Thee, and in its yearning to remember Thee and extol Thee; how it testifieth to that whereunto the Tongue of Thy Commandment hath testified in the kingdom of Thine utterance and the heaven of Thy knowledge. I love, in this state, O my Lord, to beg of Thee all that is with Thee, that I may demonstrate my poverty, and magnify Thy bounty and Thy riches, and may declare my powerlessness, and manifest Thy power and Thy might.

Let him then stand and raise his hands twice in supplication, and say:

There is no God but Thee, the Almighty, the All-Bountiful. There is no God but Thee, the Ordainer, both in the beginning and in the end . . . . O God, my God! Thy forgiveness hath emboldened me, and Thy mercy hath strengthened me, and Thy call hath awakened me, and Thy grace hath raised me up and led me unto Thee. Who, otherwise, am I that I should dare to stand at the gate of the city of Thy nearness, or set my face toward the lights that are shining from the heaven of Thy will? Thou seest, O my Lord, this wretched creature knocking at the door of Thy grace, and this evanescent soul seeking the river of everlasting life from the hands of Thy bounty . . . .

Tongue of Thy Commandment

God's commandments are a blessing

The Almighty provided guidance in His Word for the benefit of humanity. Commandments reveal the best way to live, promoting moral conduct and the development of spiritual virtues. The Self-Sufficient Creator does not benefit by our compliance with His teachings, enabling us to draw closer to the Source of our Being and live a more fulfilling life. We are the ones who profit.

Divine Revelation addresses the needs of our entire being, heart, soul, and mind. As vehicles for our training, many commands call for us to take specific actions or to refrain from specific actions. The learning is in the doing. By abiding by what God asks of us, we gain a visceral knowledge, beyond simple mental comprehension, elevating our emotional, intellectual, and spiritual make up. Hidden capacities come to fruition. We build godly habits in thought and action. Most importantly, we train ourselves to put the Giver of Life at the center of our concerns.

This is what the LORD says—Your Redeemer, the Holy One of Israel: "I am the LORD your God, who teaches you what is best for you, Who directs you in the way you should go. If only you had paid attention to my commands, Then your peace would have been like a river, your well-being like the waves of the sea." (ISAIAH 48:17–18, Hebrew scripture)

Truly, in remembering God do hearts find rest. (QUR'ÁN 13:28, Islámic scripture)

Religion is the light of the world, and the progress, achievement, and happiness of man result from obedience to the laws set down in the holy Books. ('ABDU'L-BAHÁ, *The Secret of Divine Civilization*, 7)

In what sense does God have a tongue?

In the most literal sense, God does not have a body or any body organs such as a tongue. Rather He communicates with his creatures through His spirit and prophets. The process of conveying God's will to us is described in anthropomorphic terms, using human attributes to represent spiritual realities that otherwise may be unexplainable. Thus while God has no mouth, voice box, palate or other speech organs, His communications are symbolically called His Word as if spoken by a human mouth.

> Thus hath the Tongue of Utterance spoken . . . It is now incumbent upon them who are endowed with a hearing ear and a seeing eye to ponder these sublime words, in each of which the oceans of inner meaning and explanation are hidden, that haply the words uttered by Him Who is the Lord of Revelation may enable His servants to attain, with the utmost joy and radiance . . . (BAHÁ'U'LLÁH, *Epistle to the Son of the Wolf*, 147)

. . . *demonstrate my poverty*

Here, as well as in many other Bahá'í prayers, there are parallel phases in which our powerlessness and poverty are contrasted with God's might and wealth. The contrast is the key. We may indeed have a measure of spiritual riches, pearls we have found in our exploration of the vast Ocean of Divine Revelation. However, in contrast to all that can be learned and especially in contrast with the wisdom of the infinite Lord of All, spiritually speaking we are indeed impoverished.

Spiritual poverty

> THE VALLEY OF TRUE POVERTY AND ABSOLUTE NOTHINGNESS
>
> This station is the dying from self and the living in God, the being poor in self and rich in the Desired One. Poverty as here referred to signifieth being poor in the things of the created world, rich in the things of God's world. (BAHÁ'U'LLÁH, *The Seven Valleys*, 35)

> All the wealth and glory of all creation, in comparison with the wealth which is God, is supreme poverty and wretchedness. Thus *the soul that loves and possesses creature wealth is supremely poor* (ST. JOHN OF THE CROSS, *Ascent of Mount Carmel*, Christian mystic)

Material poverty

> Poverty is highly prized by the true Muslims, because Muhammad said "Poverty is My glory." He ate sitting on the ground; His pillow was His arm; He lived in a row of modest rooms, made of sun-dried brick, furnished with leather water-bags, and leather mats stuffed with palm-

fibre, and cots of palm-fibre rope. He kindled the fire, swept the floor, patched His own garments and shoes, milked the goats. He said, "I am a servant, I eat and sleep like a servant." (MARZIEH GAIL, *Six Lessons on Islám*, 13, Bahá'í commentary)

. . . I have learned to be content whatever the circumstances. I know what it is to be in need, and I know what it is to have plenty. I have learned the secret of being content in any and every situation, whether well fed or hungry, whether living in plenty or in want. I can do all this through him who gives me strength. (PHILIPPIANS 4:11–13, Christian scripture)

Spiritual riches

From another point of view, we are rich, enjoying the abundance of God's bounteous gifts; life, a beautiful home planet, the guidance of His Word and the certitude of a glorious eternal future.

For I have created thee rich and have bountifully shed My favor upon thee. (BAHÁ'U'LLÁH, *The Arabic Hidden Words*, #11)

This is a Revelation that . . . crowneth with wealth the destitute. (BAHÁ'U'LLÁH, *Gleanings from the Writings of Bahá'u'lláh*, 183)

. . . *gate of the city of Thy nearness* . . .

City of Thy nearness

Ancient cities were places of safety, often surrounded by high, stone walls that protected the inhabitants from roaming bands of thieves and marauding armies. Entrance to the city was limited to a specific number of fortified gates, where guards monitored all comings and goings in order to keep out the dangerous and unwanted.

After the destruction of Jerusalem by the Babylonians in the sixth century BCE, Isaiah depicts a reconstruction of the city as a place of blessing, beauty and peace.

> Afflicted city, lashed by storms and not comforted,
> I will rebuild you with stones of turquoise,
> Your foundations with lapis lazuli.
> I will make your battlements of rubies,
> Your gates of sparkling jewels,
> And all your walls of precious stones.
> All your children will be taught by the LORD,
> And great will be their peace.
> (ISAIAH 54:11–13, Hebrew scripture)

The fortified City becomes a symbol of the presence of God among His people, where God's protection overshadows all. To abide in the City of God is to live one's life constantly seeking to know and do the divine will. In every street and crossroad, one sees the signs of God and rejoices in a rich, spiritual life.

> I saw the Holy City, the new Jerusalem, coming down out of heaven from God, prepared as a bride beautifully dressed for her husband. And I heard a loud voice from the throne saying, "Look! God's dwelling place is now among

the people, and he will dwell with them. They will be his
people, and God himself will be with them and be their
God. 'He will wipe every tear from their eyes. (Revelation 21:2–4, Christian scripture)

I did not see a temple in the city, because the Lord God
Almighty and the Lamb (Christ) are its temple. The city
does not need the sun or the moon to shine on it, for the
glory of God gives it light . . . . (Revelation 21:22–24,
Christian scripture)

In his famous work, *The City of God*, Augustine of Hippo uses the
image of the City to expound on the righteous life.

The glorious city of God is my theme in this work . . . I
have undertaken its defense against those who prefer their
own gods to the Founder of this city—a city surpassingly
glorious. "God resisteth the proud, but giveth grace unto
the humble." And therefore, as the plan of this work we
have undertaken requires, and as occasion offers, we must
speak also of the earthly city, which, though it be mistress
of the nations, is itself ruled by its lust of rule. (Augustine, *City of God*, Preface)

In the Bahá'í Writings, the Holy City is shown to be the Revelation
of God that affords protection and represents God's immanence.

How unspeakably glorious are the signs, the tokens, the
revelations, and splendours which He Who is the King
of names and attributes hath destined for that City! The
attainment of this City quencheth thirst without water,
and kindleth the love of God without fire.
  Wherefore, O my friend, it behooveth Us to exert the
highest endeavour to attain unto that City . . . That city

is none other than the Word of God revealed in every age and dispensation. In the days of Moses it was the Pentateuch; in the days of Jesus the Gospel; in the days of Muhammad the Messenger of God the Qur'án; in this day the Bayan; and in the dispensation of Him Whom God will make manifest His own Book . . . In these cities spiritual sustenance is bountifully provided, and incorruptible delights have been ordained. The food they bestow is the bread of heaven, and the Spirit they impart is God's imperishable blessing. Upon detached souls they bestow the gift of Unity, enrich the destitute, and offer the cup of knowledge unto them who wander in the wilderness of ignorance. All the guidance, the blessings, the learning, the understanding, the faith, and certitude, conferred upon all that is in heaven and on earth, are hidden and treasured within these Cities. (Bahá'u'lláh, *Kitáb-i-Íqán*, 195)

. . . knocking at the door of Thy grace . . .

Door of Thy grace

A door, of course, is a point of entry of a home or building. Knocking is a request to enter and visit. As seekers, we do not always know how to gain entry. A diligent search may entail knocking on the door repeatedly until we find what we seek.

> And so I tell you, keep on asking, and you will receive what you ask for. Keep on seeking, and you will find. Keep on knocking, and the door will be opened to you. (Matthew 7:7–8, Christian scripture)

> The Word is the master key for the whole world, inasmuch as through its potency the doors of the hearts of men, which in reality are the doors of heaven, are unlocked. (Baháʼuʼlláh, *Tablets of Baháʼuʼlláh*, 173)

> These are the words of him who is holy and true (Christ), who holds the key of David. What he opens no one can shut . . . (Revelation 3:7, Christian scripture)

"Door of Thy grace" is a metaphor for access to the Divine Presence. One who gains entry is blessed with the pleasure of keeping company with the Beloved as following word picture vividly describes.

> 'The door of grace hath been unlocked and He Who is the Dayspring of Justice is come with perspicuous signs and evident testimonies, from God, the Lord of strength and of might!' Present thyself before Me that thou mayest hear the mysteries which were heard by the Son of Imran

(Moses) upon the Sinai of Wisdom. (Bahá'u'lláh, *Epistle to the Son of the Wolf*, 85)

. . . river of everlasting life . . .

Rivers of Paradise

Water, especially fresh flowing water, is a universal symbol of life. In the ancient Near East, rivers like the Nile, the Euphrates, the Tigris and the Jordan took on special significance. Rivers brought fresh water from the mountainous highlands to desert areas, enabling agriculture and making the growth of civilization possible. This vital role of rivers made them an appropriate symbol of life in the sacred scriptures of all religions.

> Upon which run the many streams and rivers; upon which the many kinds of plants grow up from the ground, to nourish animals and men . . . (Zend-Avesta, Khorda Avesta, Frawardin Yashi, 10, Zoroastrian scripture)

> The Source from where Life's stream draws all waters of all rivers of all being. (Bhagavad Gita, Chapter XI, Hindu scripture)

> And a river went out of Eden to water the garden . . . (Genesis 2:10, Hebrew scripture)

> A similitude of the Garden which those who keep their duty (to Allah) are promised: Therein are rivers of water unpolluted, and rivers of milk whereof the flavour changeth not, and rivers of wine delicious to the drinkers, and rivers of clear-run honey; therein for them is every kind of fruit, with pardon from their Lord. (Qur'án 47:15, Islámic scripture)

Give me to drink of the river that is life indeed, whose waters have streamed forth from the Paradise (Riḍván) in which the throne of Thy Name . . . was established . . . (Baháʼuʼlláh, *Prayers and Meditations by Baháʼuʼlláh*, 4)

Ezekiel's Vision of Life-Giving River

Among the many visions of the Hebrew prophet, Ezekiel, was a dramatic word picture of healing waters issuing from the Throne of God. Ezekiel saw a stream flowing out of the Jerusalem Temple and running into the desert wilderness. The flow starts as a trickle but grows to a mighty river. The Dead Sea, surrounded by desert, lies in a rift valley southeast of Jerusalem. It is so salty that neither plant nor animal can survive in its briny waters. Ezekiel's river is depicted running down the mountains of Jerusalem toward the east and winding up in the Dead Sea. Miraculously the sea is revived. Fish return. Fishermen line its banks. Orchards of fruit trees thrive. What was dead becomes alive. This archetypal river pictures the power of God, who representatively resided in the Temple, to restore Israel and the world.

The Vision of Ezekiel

And he brought me back unto the door of the house (Jerusalem Temple); and, behold, waters issued out from under the threshold of the house eastward . . . Then brought he me . . . to the gate that looks toward the east; and, behold, there trickled forth waters on the right side . . . and he caused me to pass through the waters, waters that were ankle deep. Again he measured a thousand reeds downstream, and caused me to pass through the waters, waters that were up to the knees. Again he measured a thousand, and caused me to pass through waters that were to the loins. Afterward he measured a thousand; and it was a river that I could not pass through; for the waters were risen, waters to swim in, a river that could not be passed through.

. . . behold, upon the bank of the river were very many trees on the one side and on the other. Then said he unto me: 'These waters issue forth toward the eastern region, and shall go down into the Arabah Desert; and when (the waters of the Holy Temple) shall enter into the Dead Sea, into the sea of the putrid waters, the waters shall be healed.'

And it shall come to pass, that wherever the river should go, all sort of living creatures shall come to life; and there shall be a very great multitude of fish; for these waters are come there so that all things would be healed. And it shall come to pass, that fishers shall stand by . . . for the spreading of nets; their fish shall be after their kinds, as the fish of the Mediterranean Sea . . . And by the river upon the bank thereof, on this side and on that side, shall grow every tree for food, whose leaf shall not wither, neither shall the fruit thereof fail; it shall bring forth new fruit every month, because the waters thereof issue out of the sanctuary; and the fruit thereof shall be for food, and the leaf thereof for healing. (EZEKIEL 47: 1–12, Hebrew scripture)

Many of the symbols used by Ezekiel are repeated in the New Testament Book of Revelation. That book's final chapter depicts a paradise with abundant fruit trees and healing leaves. This rich literary imagery was the root of similar imagery dramatized in the Qur'án and Bahá'í scripture as seen above.

And he showed me a pure river of water of life, clear as crystal, proceeding out of the throne of God and of the Lamb . . . and on either side of the river, were trees of life, which bare twelve manner of fruits, and yielded their fruit every month: and the leaves of the trees were for the healing of the nations. (REVELATION 22:1–2, Christian scripture)

The River Jordan bringing freshwater to the Dead Sea.

SECTION 5

Too High Art Thou

Let him then raise his hands thrice, and say:

Greater is God than every great one!

Let him then kneel and, bowing his forehead to the ground, say:

Too high art Thou for the praise of those who are nigh unto Thee to ascend unto the heaven of Thy nearness, or for the birds of the hearts of them who are devoted to Thee to attain to the door of Thy gate . . . .

Let him then seat himself and say:

I testify unto that whereunto have testified all created things, and the Concourse on high, and the inmates of the all-highest Paradise, and beyond them the Tongue of Grandeur itself from the all-glorious Horizon, that Thou art God, that there is no God but Thee, and that He Who hath been manifested is the Hidden Mystery, the Treasured Symbol, through Whom the letters B and E (Be) have been joined and knit together . . . .

Let him then stand erect and say:

O Lord of all being and Possessor of all things visible and invisible! Thou dost perceive my tears and the sighs I utter, and hearest my groaning, and my wailing, and the lamentation of my heart. By Thy might! My trespasses have kept me back from drawing nigh unto Thee; and my sins have held me far from the court of Thy holiness . . . . I entreat Thee by Thy footsteps in this wilderness, and by the words "Here am I, Here am I," which Thy chosen Ones have uttered in this immensity, and by the breaths of Thy Revelation, and the gentle winds of the Dawn of Thy Manifestation, to ordain that I may gaze on Thy beauty and observe whatsoever is in Thy Book.

Too high art Thou for the praise of those who are nigh unto Thee to ascend to the Heaven of Thy nearness . . .

This phrase highlights the paradox of our relationship with our Creator. On the one hand, we worship God through prayer and service with the goal of drawing close to Him. We know from many other verses that God hears the praise, petitions, and pleadings of His servants. On the other hand, God is infinite and our finite nature limits our ability to reach Him. How are we to understand these seemingly contradictory truths?

Spiritual truths can often be best comprehended through paradox. In one sense, God is utterly distinct from the material plane, so that He is absolutely alone and unreachable. In another sense God is omniscient and knows everything that transpires in all creation. This apparent paradox serves a beneficial purpose. It presents a multifaceted view of the nature of the relationship between Creator and creature. These two truths co-exist, and their apparent contradiction helps clarify our standing.

> Wonder not, if my Best-Beloved be closer to me than mine own self; wonder at this, that I, despite such nearness, should still be so far from Him . . . (BAHÁ'U'LLÁH, *Gleanings from the Writings of Baháʼuʼlláh*, 185)

In Greek mythology, Icarus fashioned wings of feathers and wax and attempted to fly to heaven. However, when he reached a height too close to the sun, the wax melted, his wings came apart and he tumbled back to earth. This fable dramatizes human limitations.

Despite human inadequacies in comprehending and interacting with the infinite, God encourages us to get as close to Him as we possibly can. He promises that our efforts are not in vain. Nearness to God is the greatest human achievement.

> My love is in thee, know it, that thou mayest find Me near unto thee. (BAHÁ'U'LLÁH, *Arabic Hidden Words*, #. 10)

> Those hearts, however, that are aware of His Presence, are close to Him, and are to be regarded as having drawn nigh unto His throne. (BAHÁ'U'LLÁH, *Gleanings from the Writings of Baháʼuʼlláh*, 186)

. . . *birds of the hearts* . . .

Reinforcing the plain statement that God is "too high" for us to reach Him, is a metaphor of high flying birds. These "birds of the hearts" represent God's servants who are unable to fly high enough to reach the "door" of His "gate."

The word picture of seekers as birds flying the skies in search of the Beloved is an common symbol in Sufi poetry. Perhaps the most famous example is *The Conference of the Birds*, a Persian poem by Farid ud-Din Attar. In that poem, the birds of the world gather to choose a king. They determine to search for the legendary Simorgh, a wise, ancient benevolent bird to invite Him to become their king. During the quest, the character of each species of bird emerges with its own particular qualities and faults, obstacles to enlightenment. The guiding bird is the hoopoe, while the nightingale symbolizes the lover. The parrot is not interested in communion with God but selfishly seeks the fountain of immortality. The peacock is a "fallen soul" in alliance with opposers. During their arduous quest, as the birds' character faults surface, one by one they forsake the quest.

> When they had understood the hoopoe's words,
> A clamour of complaint rose from the birds . . .
> We are a wretched, flimsy crew at best,
> And lack the bare essentials for this quest.
> Our feathers and our wings, our bodies' strength.
> Are quite unequal to the journey's length . . .
> (Farid Al-Din Attar, *The Conference of the Birds*,
> Islámic poet)

When a remnant of thirty birds finally reaches the dwelling place of the Simorgh, they find not the long sought Simorgh, but a lake in which they see their own reflection. The spiritual lesson here may be that attaining the physical presence of the infinite God is a fruitless quest. All that can be known of God can be found within oneself, within the human heart.

Bird imagery depicting efforts to reach Heavenward toward the Divine is found throughout Bahá'í scripture. Holistically, this imagery is able to illustrate both the accessibility and inaccessibility of God.

O my God. Thy majesty is so transcendent that no human imagination can reach it and Thy consummate power is so sublime that the birds of men's hearts and minds can never attain its heights . . . .(THE BÁB, *Selections from the Writings of the Báb*, 194)

Blessed is the man that hath, on the wings of longing, soared towards God . . . (BAHÁ'U'LLÁH, *Epistle to the Son of the Wolf*, 94)

O God! This is a broken-winged bird and his flight is very slow—assist him so that he may fly toward the apex of prosperity and salvation, wing his way with the utmost joy and happiness throughout the illimitable space, raise his melody in Thy Supreme Name in all the regions . . . ('ABDU'L-BAHÁ, *Bahá'í Prayers*, 187)

. . . *testified all created things* . . .

This phrase marks the beginning of a series of phrases that point towards four degrees of nearness to God, Starting with "all created things," the series progresses to the "Concourse on high," the "inmates of the all-highest Paradise," and the "Tongue of Grandeur."

In what way do all created things, even inanimate objects, testify to God? All that is brought into existence by God's creative power reflects divine attributes. In the mere fact of their existence, in their form, components, structure and beauty, a sign of God is discernable.

> The Heavens declare the glory of God;
> The skies proclaim the work of his hands.
> Day after day they pour forth speech;
> Night after night they reveal knowledge.
> They have no speech, they use no words;
> No sound is heard from them.
> Yet their voice goes out into all the earth,
> Their words to the ends of the world.
> (PSALMS 19:1–4, Hebrew scripture)

> Praise belongs to God who created the heavens and the earth, and brought into being the darkness and the light.
> (QUR'ÁN 6:1, Islámic scripture)

> All the atoms of the earth proclaim Thee to be God, and testify that there is none other God besides Thee.
> (BAHÁ'U'LLÁH, *Prayers and Meditations by Bahá'u'lláh*, 241)

The spectacle of the starry heavens is superlatively beautiful. Whether we are scientists with a measure of understanding of the laws of physics or mere observers of the immensity of a star-studded sky, we cannot help but feel astonishment and wonder.

The same can be said of all created things, from the crystalline structure of rocks, to the intricate composition of plants and animals, to the marvelous design of the human body, to the particles and nuclear forces that hold each atom together. God's wisdom is on display everywhere.

. . . *Concourse on high* . . .

We often use the word "concourse" to refer to a wide open space, such as inside an airport. The word, however, can also refer to a large gathering of people and this is the sense in which it is used in the Bahá'í Writings. The phrases "Concourse on high" and "Supreme Concourse" signifying a great multitude of faithful servants of God. They are depicted circling around the divine throne representing its complete devotion to God, entrusted with the noble task of spreading the light of God in the world. As a heavenly host, they constitute a mighty army that champions the Cause of God and assures its ultimate victory.

> Know thou of a certainty that thy Lord will come to thine aid with a company of the Concourse on high and hosts of the Abhá Kingdom. These will mount the attack, and will furiously assail the forces of the ignorant, the blind . . . (ABDU'L-BAHÁ, *Selections from the Writings of 'Abdu'l-Bahá*, 43)

> . . . the Shrine (of the Báb) . . . the tomb itself housing this dust He acclaimed as the spot round which the Concourse on high circle in adoration. (SHOGHI EFFENDI, *Citadel of Faith*, 96)

Who are the members of the Concourse on High?

While it is not possible to be too specific about who its members are, Bahá'í scripture provide some specifics as well as some general statements. The Concourse on High is said to include the departed souls of the Manifestations of God and other extraordinary examples of faith.

In the Supreme Concourse are Jesus, and Moses, and Elijah, and Bahá'u'lláh, and other supreme Souls: there, also, are the martyrs." (*'Abdu'l-Bahá in London*, 97)

By God, O people! Mine eye weepeth, and the eye of Alí (the Báb) weepeth amongst the Concourse on high . . . (SHOGHI EFFENDI, *God Passes By*, 250)

In the New Testament book of Revelation, we find a symbolic vision of the Throne of God surrounded by 24 elders and thousands of angels, which vision bares some similarity to the Concourse on High.

After this I looked, and, behold, a door was opened in heaven . . . And immediately I was in the spirit: and, behold, a throne was set in heaven, and one sat on the throne . . . And round about the throne were four and twenty seats: and upon the seats I saw four and twenty elders sitting, clothed in white raiment; and they had on their heads crowns of gold. . . . And I beheld, and I heard the voice of many angels round about the throne . . . and the elders: and the number of them was ten thousand times ten thousand, and thousands of thousands; (REVELATION 4:1—5:11, Christian scripture)

Although not directly related to the wording of the Long Obligatory Prayer, the question naturally arises: Who are the twenty-four elders? Shoghi Effendi indicated that the Letters of the Living, the Báb's first eighteen disciples, are to be counted among the twenty-four elders.

Included among the twenty-four then would be the eighteen the Letters of the Living. Who then are the other six? In two tablets, the Báb named Himself as the 19th letter and He Whom God Shall Make Manifest (Bahá'u'lláh) as the 20th letter. (see Shoghi Effendi, *Unfolding Destiny*, 248).

There is no further information in Bahá'í scripture to identify the 21st, 22nd, 23rd, and 24th elders. The following list of candidates has been suggested (See *Apocalypse Secrets*, John Able, 50): 1) 'Abdu'l-Bahá, 2) Bahiyyih Khanum, Bahá'u'lláh's faithful daughter, 3) Shoghi Effendi, the Guardian, along with 4) Haji Mirza Muhammad-Taqi, a vigorous teacher of the Cause, credited with the erection of the first Bahá'í Temple in 'Ishqábád. (See 'Abdu'l-Bahá, *Memorials of the Faithful*, 126) Despite the uncertainty about the group's membership, it seems possible that this heavenly assembly of twenty-four elders are also to be included in the Concourse on High, along with many thousands of martyrs and other faithful servants of the Cause of God. They offer eternal praise before God's eternal throne.

. . . all-highest Paradise . . .

Garden of Eden prototype of Paradise

> And the LORD God planted a garden eastward in Eden;
> and there he put the man whom he had formed. And out
> of the ground made the LORD God to grow every tree
> that is pleasant to the sight, and good for food . . . And
> a river went out of Eden to water the garden. (GENESIS
> 2:8–10, Hebrew scripture)

Paradise means inner and outer peace

Bahá'ís recognize the Genesis stories of creation as non-literal sacred
revelation. Their purpose is not to reveal history but, as 'Abdu'l-
Bahá states, to convey deep spiritual lessons. When 'Abdu'l-Bahá
explains the meaning of the story of Adam and Eve, he reveals
hidden meaning in the text, showing that it contains vital lessons
about the adverse consequences of attachment to this world. (See
Some Answered Questions, 30)

> Whoso hath recognized the Day Spring of Divine guid-
> ance and entered His holy court hath drawn nigh unto
> God and attained His Presence, a Presence which is the
> real Paradise, and of which the loftiest mansions of heaven
> are but a symbol. (BAHÁ'U'LLÁH, *Gleanings from the Writ-
> ings of Bahá'u'lláh*, 70)

> The Lord of all mankind hath fashioned this human realm
> to be a Garden of Eden, an earthly paradise. If, as it must, it
> findeth the way to harmony and peace, to love and mutual
> trust, it will become a true abode of bliss . . . Remember
> how Adam and the others once dwelt together in Eden. No

sooner, however, did a quarrel break out between Adam and Satan than they were, one and all, banished from the Garden, and this was meant as a warning to the human race, a means of telling humankind that dissension—even with the Devil—is the way to bitter loss. This is why, in our illumined age, God teacheth that conflicts and disputes are not allowable, not even with Satan himself. ('Abdu'l-Bahá, *Selections from the Writings of 'Abdu'l-Bahá*, 275)

'Abdu'l-Bahá's words regarding Satan in the above quote show us an important fact about the way he taught. From other passages, we know that 'Abdu'l- Bahá did not believe in a literal devil with whom Adam could dispute. Nevertheless, he took the story at face value and made a spiritual point **without** being distracted by discussion of whether the Devil is literal or symbolic in this context.

If we look upon a soul as rejected, we have disobeyed the teachings of God. God is loving to all . . . Shall we manifest hatred for His creatures and servants? This would be contrary to the will of God and according to the will of Satan, by which we mean the natural inclinations of the lower nature. This lower nature in man is symbolized as Satan—the evil ego within us, not an evil personality outside. ('Abdu'l-Bahá, *The Promulgation of Universal Peace*, 287)

God is the Father of all; there is not a single exception to that law. There are no people of Satan; all belong to the Merciful. ('Abdu'l-Bahá, *The Promulgation of Universal Peace*, 266)

Paradise and Hell are symbols

They say: 'Where is Paradise, and where is Hell?' Say: 'The one is reunion with Me; the other thine own self . . . (Bahá'u'lláh, *Epistle to the Son of the Wolf*, 132)

> Existential paradise and hell are to be found in all the
> worlds of God, whether in this world or in the heavenly
> realms of spirit . . . ('ABDU'L-BAHÁ, *Some Answered Ques-*
> *tions*, 60, 2)

The tree of life in the Garden of Eden is the Word of God, the source
of spiritual food. This food originates in the heavenly realm of the
Manifestations of God, here called the "all- Highest Paradise."

> By "the tree of life" is meant the highest degree of the world
> of existence, that is, the station of the Word of God and
> His universal Manifestation. That station was indeed well
> guarded, until it appeared and shone forth in the supreme
> revelation of His universal Manifestation. For the station of
> Adam, with regard to the appearance and manifestation of
> the divine perfections, was that of the embryo; the station
> of Christ was that of coming of age and maturation; and
> the dawning of the Most Great Luminary (Bahá'u'lláh) was
> the station of the perfection of the essence and the attri-
> butes. That is why in the all-highest Paradise the tree of life
> alludes to the focal centre of absolute sanctity and purity,
> that is, the universal Manifestation of God. ('ABDU'L-
> BAHÁ, *Some Answered Questions*, 30, 7)

The Lote-Tree

In Islámic tradition, the Lote-Tree is a desert tree marking the end
of the road. It came to symbolize the impassible limit between the
physical and spiritual worlds, a barrier beyond which no human can
cross.

In the (Qur'án 17), the Lote Tree is called the "utmost boundary." There the Prophet received revelation, and so it can also represent a meeting point between the physical and spiritual realms.

And He revealed unto His slave that which He revealed . . .
By the Lote-Tree of the utmost boundary,
Nigh unto which is the Garden of Abode.
(Qur'án 53:10–15, Islámic scripture)

As the connection between the realms of God and the realms of humanity, the Lote Tree represents revelation and also the revelator, the Manifestations of God.

> These sublime words were heard today from the rustling of the divine Lote-Tree which the Lord of Names hath, with the hand of celestial power, planted in the All-Highest Paradise: (Bahá'u'lláh, *Tablets of Bahá'u'lláh*, 34)

> The Sacred Lote-Tree, the Tree beyond which there is no passing (See Qur'án 53:8–18). A symbol of the Manifestation of God. (Footnote from *Tablets of Bahá'u'lláh*, 209)

. . . all-glorious Horizon . . .

Horizon

In flat landscapes, whether plains or ocean, the horizon is a perfect circle marking the place where the sky and earth meet. In hilly and mountainous areas, the circle is warped but, nevertheless, at sunrise forms a sharp boundary between light and shadow. The dawning points of each new day lie along that line.

All-Glorious

The phrase "all-glorious" occurs three times in the Long Obligatory Prayer. On the other two occasions it is coupled with the parallel name of God, the "Most Exalted." Here, it stands alone as an indication that the spiritual horizon is adorned with the beauty of the appearance of the Manifestation of God. All eyes wonder at the spectacular display of a sunrise, as the sky transforms second by second into a fiery flash that announces the beginning of a new day. This inevitable cycle of transformation provides a fitting picture of the impact of the Promised One from age to age.

> The great spiritual lights have always appeared in the East. The Blessed Perfection, Bahá'u'lláh, appeared in the East. Jesus Christ dawned upon the horizon of the East. Moses, Aaron, Joseph and all the Israelitish prophets such as Jeremiah, Ezekiel, Isaiah and others appeared from the Orient. The lights of Muhammad and the Báb shone from the East. The eastern horizon has been flooded with the effulgence of these great lights, and only from the East have they risen to shine upon the West. Now—praise be to God!—you are living in the dawn of a cycle when the Sun of Truth is

again shining forth from the East, illumining all regions.
('ABDU'L-BAHÁ, *The Promulgation of Universal Peace*, 23)

This multifaceted analogy goes deeper, as it addresses the misguided view that the supreme diety of the various world religions are not the same God. Due to seasonal cycles, the sun comes up at different points on the horizon each day of the year. The Spring Equinox, the Summer Solstice, The Fall Equinox and the Winter Solstice divide the cycle of change into four distinct periods.

Each sunrise is unique, as cloud patterns spread dawn colors in diverse textures. Yet the sun is still the same sun. The changes in the compass points of its rising are merely transient aspects of the same heavenly body.

> The Sun of Reality is one Sun, but it has different dawning places, just as the phenomenal sun is one although it appears at various points of the horizon. During the time of summer the luminary of the physical world rises far to the north of the equinoctial, in spring and fall it dawns midway, and in winter it appears in the most southerly point of its zodiacal journey. These daysprings or dawning points differ widely, but the sun is ever the same sun—whether it be the phenomenal or spiritual luminary. Souls who focus their vision upon the Sun of Reality will be the recipients of light no matter from what point it rises, but those who are fettered by adoration of the dawning point are deprived when it appears in a different station upon the spiritual horizon. ('ABDU'L-BAHÁ, *The Promulgation of Universal Peace*, 94)

As the dawning point of the sun goes through these various stages, so do the stars. The twelve constellations of the Zodiac move around the sky in an annual cycle. Thus if the constellation Gemini rises in the eastern sky at dawn, the sun is said to be in Gemini. Likewise with Pieces, Leo and all the constellations of the Zodiac. By describing the varying dawning points with reference to the signs of the Zodiac, 'Abdu'l-Bahá may be alluding to the various cultural and historical environments in which each Manifestation appeared, even though it is the same sun rising regardless the location or time. Similarly, the same voice of God speaks in each revelation, regardless of the name of the Manifestation of God of that age or the cultural climate in which it appears. The source of all such light, veiled or clear, red, orange or yellow, is identical.

> The spiritual cycles of the Sun of Truth, like the cycles of the physical sun, are in a state of perpetual motion and renewal. The Sun of Truth can be likened to the material sun, which rises from many different points. One day it rises from the sign of Cancer and another from the sign of Libra; one day it casts its rays from the sign of Aquarius and another from that of Aries. Yet the sun is but one sun and one single reality. The possessors of true knowledge are lovers of the sun and are not attached to its dawning points . . . Thus they bow in adoration before the sun, from whatever sign and above whatever horizon it may appear, and seek the truth from any sanctified soul who might reveal it. ('ABDU'L-BAHÁ, *Some Answered Questions*, 14, 12)

. . . He who hath been Manifested is the Hidden Mystery

As Bahá'u'lláh explains at length in *Kitáb-i-Íqán*, the Manifestations of God possess a two-fold station, the station of unity and the station of distinction. The station of unity entails a mystical connection outside of time, wherein all Manifestations of God are one in every respect, none is greater or lesser than the other, none is before or after another.

> These Manifestations of God have each a twofold station. One is the station of pure abstraction and essential unity. In this respect, if thou callest them all by one name, and dost ascribe to them the same attribute, thou hast not erred from the truth. (BAHÁ'U'LLÁH, *Kitáb-i-Íqán*, 152)

In the station of distinction, each Manifestation possesses an individual identity. They each have a human body, unique personalities and names. They each live and die in the physical world at a specific time in history, have a specific role to play in the advancement of civilization.

> . . . the station of distinction . . . pertaineth to the world of creation and to the limitations thereof. In this respect, each Manifestation of God hath a distinct individuality, a definitely prescribed mission, a predestined Revelation, and specially designated limitations. Each one of them is known by a different name, is characterized by a special attribute, fulfills a definite Mission, and is entrusted with a particular Revelation. (BAHÁ'U'LLÁH, *Kitáb-i-Íqán*, 176)

This two-fold stations is an eternal paradox, for how can anyone have two identities simultaneously, one temporal and knowable, the other non-temporal and unknowable. This mystical reality is possible only through God's grace, which can be called a "third station."

> O Thou Who art the most manifest of the manifest and the most hidden of the hidden! (BAHÁ'U'LLÁH, *Prayers and Meditations by Bahá'u'lláh*, 248)

> The third station is that of divine grace . . . The individual realities of the holy Manifestations cannot be separated from divine grace . . . The Manifestations of God are like so many different mirrors, as They each have Their own distinct individuality, but that which is reflected in these mirrors is one and the same sun. Thus, it is evident that the reality of Christ is different from that of Moses. ('ABDU'L-BAHÁ, *Some Answered Questions*, 39, 4)

Although the term "two-fold station," is found only in Bahá'í scripture, the concept is found other sacred books. For example, Abdu'l Baha points of a similar theme in the Christian New Testament.

> Such is the case of Christ's coming from heaven. It has been explicitly stated in numerous passages of the Gospel that the Son of man came down from heaven, or is in heaven, or will go up to heaven. Thus in John 6:38 it is said: "For I came down from heaven," and in John 6:42 it is recorded: "And they said, Is not this Jesus, the son of Joseph, whose father and mother we know? how is it then that he saith, I came down from heaven?," and in John 3:13 it is stated: "And no man hath ascended up to heaven, but He that came down from heaven, even the Son of man which is in heaven."
>
> Consider how it is said that the Son of man is in heaven, even though at that time Christ was dwelling upon the earth. ('ABDU'L-BAHÁ, *Some Answered Questions*, 23, 3–4)

This same dichotomy is true of all Manifestations of God including Moses, Zoroaster, Buddha, Christ, Muhammad, the White Buffalo Calf Woman, and Bahá'u'lláh. This perspective is essential to the unity of all religions. Otherwise, the later revelations and the religions founded on them would be seen as inferior to those that came later.

> As to the matter of names, Muhammad, Himself, declared: "I am Jesus." He recognized the truth of the signs, prophecies, and words of Jesus, and testified that they were all of God. In this sense, neither the person of Jesus nor His writings hath differed from that of Muhammad and of His Holy Book, inasmuch as both have championed the Cause of God, uttered His praise, and revealed His commandments. (BAHÁ'U'LLÁH, *Gleanings from the Writings of Bahá'u'lláh*, 21)

'Abdu'l-Bahá elaborated further on this theme, explaining how the Manifestations of God each possess a personal soul that, like all of the human souls, survives the death of the body. Thus the Manifestations are not the reincarnation of one divine being, but retain their individuality after death.

> It is therefore evident that the Manifestations of God have three stations: the physical station, the station of the rational soul, and the station of divine manifestation and heavenly splendour. The corporeal station will inevitably perish. As to the station of the rational soul, despite having a beginning, it has no end and is endowed with everlasting life. ('ABDU'L-BAHÁ, *Some Answered Questions*, 38, 8)

> In the Supreme Concourse are Jesus, and Moses, and Elijah, and Bahá'u'lláh, and other supreme Souls . . . " (*'Abdu'l-Bahá in London*, 97)

Thus the message of the Manifestations has a superlative-power. It transforms the planet, although they may remain unaware of its effect each new revelation impacts everyone, believers and non-believers alike,. The essence of the Manifestations and their means of transforming the world in both visible and invisible ways constitutes another aspect of God's sovereign governance of humankind.

.

. . . *letters B and E (Be) have been joined and knit together.*

The creative power of God is demonstrated in the opening chapter of the Hebrew Bible. When God creates, He merely utters the work "Be!" and His work is done.

Here the word "be" itself is shown to be a creation formed by joining its constituent letters. When "B" and "E" (in English) are joined, they are not merely set side by side, but are "knit" together, forming a single, compound entity, epitomizing God's creative power in one word.

> My Lord Who, through a single word of His Mouth, hath brought into being all created things! (Bahá'u'lláh, *The Summons of the Lord of Hosts*, 167)

> Arise, and serve Him Who is the Desire of all nations, Who hath created you through a word from Him . . . (Bahá'u'lláh, *The Proclamation of Bahá'u'lláh*, 5)

The original language of this prayer is Arabic. "B" and "E" are translations. What, then, are the equivalent letters in Arabic that are joined and knit together in the creation command?

> Shoghi Effendi, in letters written on his behalf, has explained the significance of the "letters B and E." They constitute the word "Be," which, he states, "means the creative Power of God Who through His command causes all things to come into being." The imperative "Be" in the original Arabic is the word "kun," consisting of the two letters "kaf" and "nun." They have been translated by Shoghi Effendi in the above manner. This word has been used in the Qur'án as God's bidding calling creation into being. (Notes to *The Kitáb-i-Aqdas*, 247)

The Power of Letters

This concept of creation by the command of God is a common thread that runs through the Bible, the Qur'án and other sacred texts. Like atoms joining together to create molecular compounds, so are the inherent power of letters are joined to fashion something new, often very different from the characteristics of their constituent parts.

> And God said, Let there **be** light: and there was light . . . And God said, Let there be lights in the firmament of the heaven to divide the day from the night . . . (GENESIS 1:3, 14, Hebrew scripture)

> The Originator of the heavens and the earth! When He decreeth a thing, He saith unto it only: Be! (Arabic: *kun*) and it is. (QUR'ÁN 2:117, Islámic scripture)

> He divided himself threefold, for Om consists of three letters, a+u+m. Through them all this is contained in him as warp and woof. For thus it is said: 'Meditate on your Self (the breath) with the (Self of the) Sun.' (UPANISHAD, Sixth Prapatraka, 3, Hindu scripture)

My trespasses have kept me back from drawing nigh unto Thee

Bahá'u'lláh gives us insight into another veil that can interfere with our effort to draw close to God. Whether due to shame, feelings of unworthiness or a troubled conscience, those who act contrary to God's law often feel reticent to approach Him in prayer.

In a well-known passage in *Kitáb-i-Íqán* (known informally as the Tablet of the True Seeker), Bahá'u'lláh provides more specifics on behaviors that encumber relationships with the Divine. A primary requirement is a heart that is open to divine guidance. A wide range of behaviors are listed, any of which can hinder an individual from drawing nigh unto Him.

> But, O my brother, when a true seeker determineth to take the step of search in the path leading to the knowledge of the Ancient of Days, he must, before all else, cleanse and purify his heart . . . He must never seek to exalt himself above any one, must wash away from the tablet of his heart every trace of pride and vainglory . . . refrain from idle talk. . . . regard backbiting as grievous error . . . be freed from all inordinate desire . . . regard avoidance of boastful and worldly people a precious benefit . . . . succour the dispossessed, and never withhold his favour from the destitute . . . show kindness to animals, how much more unto his fellow-man . . . nor allow the censure of the people to turn him away from the Truth . . . . He should forgive the sinful, and never despise his low estate . . . (BAHÁ'U'LLÁH, *Kitáb-i-Íqán*, 192)

Similarly, 'Abdu'l-Bahá lists personality traits and behaviors that block or hinder the search of God.

> Evil is imperfection. Sin is the state of man in the world of
> the baser nature, for in nature exist defects such as injus-
> tice, tyranny, hatred, hostility, strife: these are characteris-
> tics of the lower plane of nature. These are the sins of the
> world . . . Through education we must free ourselves from
> these imperfections. The Prophets of God have been sent,
> the Holy Books have been written, so that man may be
> made free. ('Abdu'l-Bahá, *Paris Talks*, 177)

Despite whatever sinful past or present tendencies the honest hearted
seeker is forced to deal with, she / he is assured of God's great mercy.

> Verily, the breezes of forgiveness have been wafted from
> the direction of your Lord, the God of Mercy; whoso tur-
> neth thereunto, shall be cleansed of his sins, and of all pain
> and sickness. Happy the man that hath turned towards
> them . . . (Bahá'u'lláh, *Epistle to the Son of the Wolf*, 46)

Embracing godly conduct means making changes in thought, word
and action to align ourselves every more closely with God's commandments. Acting to do God's will opens the gate for a stronger
relationship with Him.

Thy footsteps in this wilderness . . .

A wilderness is a barren landscape, void of civilization. The image of God walking in the wilderness signifies that He can be found away from the madding crowd, separate from the ordinary concerns of everyday society.

> All the Embodiments of His Names wander in the wilderness of search, athirst and eager to discover His Essence . . . (BAHÁ'U'LLÁH, *Gleanings from the Writings of Bahá'u'lláh*, 61)

Many prophets of old distanced themselves from the population centers of their day. They spent time in the wilderness, seeking the quiet of sparsely settled deserts or forests, avoiding the distractions of the world and focusing on spiritual reality. Among prominent examples of spiritual teachers who sought self-imposed isolation are Moses and Elijah in the Sinai desert, Buddha living as a hermit in the forest, John the Baptist in the arid lands east of the Jordan River, Jesus on his 40-day fast, Muhammad in the Hira cave near Mecca and Bahá'u'lláh in solitude in the mountains of Kurdistan.

Trekking in the wilderness requires leaving behind conveniences of cities and civilization such as soft beds, greater variety of food, companionship, protection, etc. The efforts of the followers of the Prophets to walk in their footsteps through harsh terrain depicts detachment from all save God. The difficulties encountered in uninhabited hot, dry, or mountainous terrains elicit determination in the seeker to persevere toward the mystical goal despite all obstacles and dangers.

Bahá'u'lláh describes the spiritual experience of solitude

> We betook Ourselves to the wilderness, and there, separated and alone, led for two years a life of complete solitude. From Our eyes there rained tears of anguish, and

in Our bleeding heart there surged an ocean of agonizing pain. Many a night We had no food for sustenance, and many a day Our body found no rest. By Him Who hath My being between His hands! notwithstanding these showers of afflictions and unceasing calamities, Our soul was wrapt in blissful joy, and Our whole being evinced an ineffable gladness. For in Our solitude We were unaware of the harm or benefit, the health or ailment, of any soul. Alone, We communed with Our spirit, oblivious of the world and all that is therein. (BAHÁ'U'LLÁH, *Kitáb-i-Íqán*, 250)

Wilderness of encounter

Were they to discover the sweetness of Thy remembrance . . . they would cast away all that they possess, and would rush forth into the wilderness of their longing after Thee, that the glance of Thy loving-kindness may be directed towards them . . . (BAHÁ'U'LLÁH, *Prayers and Meditations by Bahá'u'lláh*, 201)

Footsteps

. . . that My servants may follow in Thy footsteps, and be of them who are guided aright. (BAHÁ'U'LLÁH, *The Summons of the Lord of Hosts*, 37)

Thy word is a lamp unto my feet, and a light unto my path. (PSALMS 199:105, Hebrew scripture)

I follow in the footsteps of those who enjoy the Love of my Beloved. I beg of them, I implore them; I have such a yearning to meet God! (SIREE RAAG, 28, Sikh scripture)

. . . the breaths of Thy Revelation and the gentle winds of the Dawn of Thy Manifestation . . .

Two parallel images describing the advent of the Word of God are here juxtaposed. Speech involves movement of air around teeth, tongue, and throat. Dawn is accompanied by gentle breezes as the rising sun warms the air and causes it to rise. Both images relate to the movement of air that is destined to have a transformative effect on the world.

In both Hebrew and Arabic the words for "wind" and "spirit" are related. (Hebrew: *ruach*. Arabic:, *ryh, rwh.*) Wind and spirit are both invisible forces symbolically representing the Spirit of God.

Breath

> It has been promised and recorded in all the Sacred Books and Scriptures that in this Day of God His divine and spiritual sovereignty will be established, the world will be renewed, a fresh spirit will be breathed into the body of creation . . . . ('ABDU'L-BAHÁ, *Some Answered Questions*, 11, 35)

> . . . a single breath from the breezes of the Day of Thy Revelation is enough to adorn all mankind with a fresh attire. (BAHÁ'U'LLÁH, *Epistle to the Son of the Wolf*, 10)

Air movement is often associated with God's life-giving work in the world. The stage of preparation, prior to the creation of the world is thus described:

> And the Spirit of God moved upon the face of the waters. (GENESIS 1:2, Hebrew scripture)

Like the radiant sun is Krishna midst the planets of the sky, Sunless climes are warmed to verdure by the sun's returning ray, Windless wastes are waked to gladness when reviving breezes play, (MABABHARATA IV, Hindu scripture)

Gentle winds

God's creative winds are called "gentle" for a reason. God's messages are mild. They come to this world, not as overpowering storms, but as gentle breezes, which only the discerning detect. God's gentle ways of dealing with His creatures signifies the nurturing nature of His loving care.

I implore Thee by . . . gentle winds of Thy bountiful grace passed over all created things, to graciously assist me, at all times and under all conditions, to serve Thy Cause, and to enable me to remember Thee and to extol Thy virtues. (BAHÁ'U'LLÁH, *Prayers and Meditations by Bahá'u'lláh*, 227)

Ever since the day Thou didst create me and didst arouse me through the gentle winds of Thy tender mercies, I have refused to turn to anyone except Thee . . . (BAHÁ'U'LLÁH, *Prayers and Meditations by Bahá'u'lláh*, 301)

SECTION 6

Thou Hast Aided Me to Remember Thee

*Let him then repeat the Greatest Name thrice,
and bend down with hands resting on the knees,
and say:*

Praise be to Thee, O my God, that Thou hast aided
me to remember Thee and to praise Thee . . .

Let him then rise and say:

O God, my God! My back is bowed by the burden
of my sins, and my heedlessness hath destroyed me.
Whenever I ponder my evil doings and Thy benevolence, my heart melteth within me, and my blood
boileth in my veins . . . .

*Let him then repeat the Greatest Name thrice,
and kneel with his forehead to the ground, and
say:*

Praise be unto Thee, O our God, that Thou hast sent
down unto us that which draweth us nigh unto Thee,
and supplieth us with every good thing sent down by
Thee in Thy Books and Thy Scriptures. Protect us,
we beseech Thee, O my Lord, from the hosts of idle
fancies and vain imaginations. Thou, in truth, art the
Mighty, the All-Knowing.

*Let him then raise his head, and seat himself,
and say:*

I testify, O my God, to that whereunto Thy chosen
Ones have testified, and acknowledge that which
the inmates of the all-highest Paradise and those
who have circled round Thy mighty Throne have
acknowledged. The kingdoms of earth and heaven
are Thine, O Lord of the worlds!

... *my heart melteth within me and my blood boileth in my veins* ...

Here we have another pair of symbols that amplify each other,
"hearts melt" and "blood boils." The surrounding verses, both before
and after this phrase, dramatize the internal turmoil of those who
seeks to do God's will, yet finds themselves unable to live up to its
lofty standards; "Whenever I ponder my evil doings" and "my longing hands are ashamed to stretch forth toward the heaven of Thy
Bounty." Being detached from the things of this world, suppressing
all ego-driven emotions may prove to be extraordinarily difficult.
Even those believers who have achieved a measure of success are
overwhelmed by the contrast with the purity of the righteousness,
the tact, the kindness, the justice, the capacity of the Manifestation
to transform souls.

So I find it to be a law that when I want to do what is good,
evil lies close at hand. For I delight in the law of God in

my inmost self, but I see in my members another law at war with the law of my mind, making me captive to the law of sin that dwells in my members. (ROMANS 7:21–23, Christian scripture)

Thou well knowest that Mine heart hath melted in Thy Cause, and that My blood so boileth in My veins with the fire of Thy love that every drop of it proclaimeth with its inner tongue: "Grant that I may be spilt upon the ground for Thy sake, O my Lord, . . ." (BAHÁ'U'LLÁH, *The Summons of the Lord of Hosts*, 104)

. . . *every good thing sent down by Thee in Thy Books and Thy Scriptures . . .*

Those who are through struggle and perseverance are able to attain the presence of God's Messengers gain the unique privilege of hearing the Word of God directly from the mouth of the Prophet. However, most of us rely on "books" and "scriptures," the written word in order to "hear" the divine message.

The wisdom and teachings of multitude of ancient prophets who did not leave books has been largely lost or distorted. While orally transmitted teachings can be powerful and transformative, they are also subject to change over time based on intentional or unintentional rewording or alteration. While not foolproof, the written word is a more trustworthy method of textual transmission, less prone to change from one copy to the next or one generation to the next. A study of the differences between manuscripts of both the Hebrew Bible (Christian Old Testament) and the New Testament shows most variants are in spelling or changes in word order, generally easily recognized and corrected. For good reason, books and scriptures are deemed a more reliable method of preserving the message of the prophets.

> We have also heard a number of the foolish of the earth assert that the genuine text of the heavenly Gospel doth not exist amongst the Christians, that it hath ascended unto heaven. How grievously they have erred! . . . What law could be their stay and guide? . . . We take refuge with God, from that which His creatures have fancied about Him! Exalted is He above their comprehension! (BAHÁ'U'LLÁH, *Kitáb-i-Íqán*, 87)

Good things

> The Spirit breathing through the Holy Scriptures is food
> for all who hunger. God Who has given the revelation to
> His Prophets will surely give of His abundance daily bread
> to all those who ask Him faithfully. ('ABDU'L-BAHÁ, *Paris
> Talks*, 56)

Thy Books and Thy Scriptures

Bahá'ís understand that God has revealed His will at various times
and through various prophets to all the peoples of the world.

> Once in about a thousand years shall this City be renewed
> and re-adorned . . . Wherefore, O my friend, it behooveth
> Us to exert the highest endeavour to attain unto that City . . .
> That city is none other than the Word of God revealed in
> every age and dispensation. In the days of Moses it was the
> Pentateuch; in the days of Jesus the Gospel; in the days of
> Muhammad the Messenger of God the Qur'án; in this day
> the Bayan; and in the dispensation of Him Whom God will
> make manifest His own Book—the Book unto which all the
> Books of former Dispensations must needs be referred . . .
> (BAHÁ'U'LLÁH, *Kitáb-i-Íqán*, 198)

Nevertheless, the revealed words as contained in the now existing scriptures of the various religions may be of varying reliability. Bahá'ís recognize accuracy of the preserved writings of the Báb and Bahá'u'lláh.
Concerning the Qur'án, "there is no uncertainty." For Bahá'ís, the Bible
is considered to be generally authentic, although some inaccuracies,
including transmission errors and later additions are acknowledged.
Zoroastrian, Hindu, and Buddhist scriptures are likewise recognized
to contain teachings of their founding Prophets, despite historical or
textual problems.

God sent His Prophets into the world to teach and enlighten man, to explain to him the mystery of the Power of the Holy Spirit, to enable him to reflect the light, and so in his turn, to be the source of guidance to others. **The Heavenly Books, the Bible, the Qur'án, and the other Holy Writings have been given by God as guides into the paths of Divine virtue**, love, justice and peace. ('ABDU'L-BAHÁ, *Paris Talks*, 61–2)

When 'Abdu'l-Bahá states we believe what is in the Bible, He means in substance. Not that we believe every word of it to be taken literally or that every word is the authentic saying of the Prophet. (From a letter written on behalf of the Guardian to an individual believer and cited on behalf of the House of Justice, March 13, 1986 in a letter to an individual believer)

These things are recorded in the Torah, or Old Testament, in the Gospel, the Qur'án, the Zend- Avesta (Zoroastrian scripture), the books of Buddha and the book of Confucius. In brief, **all the Holy Books contain these glad tidings**. They announce that after the world is surrounded by darkness, radiance shall appear. ('ABDU'L-BAHÁ, *The Promulgation of Universal Peace*, 220)

A comparison of manuscripts of the ancient holy books and other chronological considerations indicates that the words of Moses, Zoroaster, Christ, the Buddha and other prophets have not been transmitted with precise accuracy. Over time, doctrines and practices have evolved among their followers including changes and additions to their respective books that, to varying degrees, obscures the original teachings of these great spiritual educators. Too often the accretions of time result in disunity, superiority claims and antagonism toward other belief systems. Nevertheless, the Bahá'í scriptures assure us that the essence of the teachings of these ancient prophets have been preserved. Their elevating influence continues to provide spiritual guidance to millions.

> The light of Christ is evident. The candle of Buddha is shining. The star of Moses is sparkling. The flame ignited by Zoroaster is still burning. ('ABDU'L-BAHÁ, *The Promulgation of Universal Peace*, 346)

> In spite of their historical and textual problems, the writings of the previous religions are to be counted among "Thy books and Thy scriptures." In practice, this means that they can be used in Bahá'í worship, such as in the devotional portion of Feast (*Lights of Guidance*, 2d ed., 821) or in public programs at a Bahá'í House of Worship (*Lights of Guidance*, 2d ed., 607).

If we are to fully receive the good things that are sent down to us in the Sacred Scriptures, we must study to understand their deep spiritual meaning. Many fail in this regard by misunderstanding spiritual language and mistaking it for literal everyday speech.

> The Holy Books have their special terminologies which must be known and understood. Physicians have their own peculiar terms; architects, philosophers have their characteristic expressions; poets have their phrases; and scientists, their nomenclature. In the scripture we read that Zion is dancing. It is evident that this has other than literal interpretation. The meaning is that the people of Zion shall rejoice . . . . Again in scriptures it is said, "The trees of the field shall clap their hands." This is symbolical. ('ABDU'L-BAHÁ, *The Promulgation of Universal Peace*, 246)

. . . the hosts of idle fancies and vain imaginations.

Hosts

A host represents a large number. "The hosts of heaven," for example, refers to thousands of stars. A host of idle fancies refers to more than an occasional misunderstanding, but implies numerous mistaken views that add error to error.

Idle fancies

In the realm of religion it is quite common for believers to hold on to traditional beliefs without reexamining their truth. Strongly held beliefs can be either misunderstandings of scripture or teachings that were once appropriate, but now have become outdated Therefore "idle fancies" are beliefs without spiritual merit or benefit that distract from, rather than draw one to, divine truth.

Vain imaginations

Idle fancies and vain imaginations are synonymous expressions showing the futility of certain patterns of belief. There are, of course, many different kinds of erroneous ideas, but in a spiritual context, certain misconceptions are specifically misleading. Among them are literal understandings of spiritual verses and following familiar patterns of thought and behavior while failing to recognize newly revealed truths. A recognition of God's Sovereignty requires that we be willing to readjust our thinking.

O people of God! In this day everyone should fix his eyes upon the horizon of these blessed words: 'Alone and unaided He doeth whatsoever He pleaseth.' Whoso attaineth this station hath verily attained the light of the essential unity of God and is enlightened thereby, while all others are reckoned in the Book of God among the followers of idle fancy and vain imagination. (BAHÁ'U'LLÁH, *Tablets of Bahá'u'lláh*, 96)

Chief among vain imaginings that block people from spiritual growth is adherence to the lamp rather than the light. Over time, believers can become overly attached to the sayings of their founding Prophet, fancying He has brought the final Word and consequently that the bounty of Divine Revelation has permanently ended.

It is evident that the changes brought about in every Dispensation constitute the dark clouds that intervene between the eye of man's understanding and the Divine Luminary which shineth forth from the day spring of the Divine Essence. Consider how men for generations have been blindly imitating their fathers, and have been trained according to such ways and manners as have been laid down by the dictates of their Faith . . . (BAHÁ'U'LLÁH, *Gleanings from the Writings of Bahá'u'lláh*, 26)

. . . *those who have circled round Thy mighty Throne . . .*

Circumambulating or walking in a circle around a sacred space is a way of demonstrating the special potency of that place. Native Americans circumambulate sacred fire. Some Hindu, Buddhist, Jewish, Christian, and Sikh practices include walking in circles or circumambulating an object. The Kaaba in Mecca is believed to be the most circumambulated structure in the world. Bahá'ís similarly walk around the Shrines of the Báb and Bahá'u'lláh.

> These are they who circle round the Cause of God even as the shadow doth revolve around the sun. (BAHÁ'U'LLÁH, *The Summons of the Lord of Hosts*, 9)

This physical act has great significance. It is a sign that we place the divine at the center of our lives. That everything we do or say revolves around God. While living in this physical world, those who serve God are said to circumambulate His Throne through righteous inclinations, virtuous conduct and service.

> Hasten forth and circumambulate the City of God that hath descended from heaven, the celestial Kaaba round which have circled in adoration the favored of God, the pure in heart, and the company of the most exalted angels. Oh, how I long to announce unto every spot on the surface of the earth, and to carry to each one of its cities, the glad-tidings of this Revelation (BAHÁ'U'LLÁH, *Gleanings from the Writings of Bahá'u'lláh*, 16)

> Whensoever, in sleep, I call to mind and see thy smiling face, whensoever, by day or night, I circumambulate thine honoured tomb . . . (*Compilations, From the Writings of Shoghi Effendi*, III, Bahíyyih Khánum, 53)

Since the City of God is understood to represent the Holy Books, circling around them is a symbolic way of stating our appreciation of their divine messages, as we make the written word our inspiration and guide. These symbolic acts often are actions of the heart. Circumambulating in one's sleep is not sleepwalking. Rather it is a mental condition. The revealed principle is that day and night our inner life is wrapped around divine concerns. God is "all things above all things."

SECTION 7

Themes

The central purpose of the Long Obligatory Prayer is to cement and expand the relationship between the one praying and God. Various expressions and aspects of that divine relationship are enumerated in the prayer, often repeated in parallel or synonymous phrases that reinforce each other and give a variety of perspectives.

Some examples of phrases in the Long Obligatory Prayer relating to specific spiritual themes are listed below. This list is not intended to be exhaustive. You, the reader, will no doubt, be able to add to the lists as you continue to study and reflect on the spiritual lessons contained in this prayer.

God's Oneness

No God is there but Thee

God's Kingship

Thou Who rulest over all men
Thine is the authority to command
The kingdoms of earth and heaven are Thine
Lord of the Throne on high and of earth below
The Kingdom of thine utterance
King of the seen and the unseen Lord of the worlds
Thy sovereignty
Thy mighty Throne
The court of Thy glory
The court of Thy holiness

Divine Qualities

All-Glorious
Most Exalted
Thy benevolence
The Compassionate

Thy forgiveness
Thy grace
Thy grandeur
Thy majesty
Thy mercy
Thou hast been sanctified above all attributes
Most Merciful
God of grace to the wicked.

Humanity's yearning for nearness to God

Desire of the World
This stranger hastening to his most exalted home
To stand at the gate of the city of Thy nearness
Knocking at the door of Thy grace

Oneness of Humanity

All are His servants

Oneness of Religion

Maker of the Heavens (of Divine Revelation)

Humility

This lowly creature
I am Thy servant
Standing ready to do Thy will and Thy desire
I have desired only what Thou didst desire
Mine is resignation and willing submission to Thy will

SECTION 8

"Out of Jewish Roots"

Reprinted from Lights of 'Irfán Book Seven

This paper, given at the Irfan Colloquia at Louhelen Bahá'í Center in 2006 and subsequently published in *Lights of 'Irfan*, contains a study of the progressive development of prayer in the Abrahamic tradition. This perspective may be valuable to students of the Long Obligatory Prayer by setting this prayer in historical context in relation to Judaism, Christianity, Islam, and the Bahá'í Faith.

Out of Jewish Roots

Studies of Prayer Patterns in Jewish,
Christian, Muslim and Bahá'í Worship

TED BROWNSTEIN

Abstract

Daily prayer is one of the essential practices of the Abrahamic religions. Some of the progressive elements of this
series of revelations are demonstrated by this paper as an
exploration of the development of liturgy and personal
prayer patterns from its roots in Judaism and subsequent
development in Christianity, Islam and the Bahá'í Faith.

Introduction

Progressive revelation is central to Bahá'í theology. It is the bedrock
upon which belief in the fundamental unity of religion is built, as it
provides a conceptual basis for seeing the interconnections between
the world's diverse religions. All are seen as equally valid paths to

God. At the same time each is seen as a spiritual advancement, built upon the traditions and successes of its predecessors.

> . . . in accordance with the principle of progressive rev-
> elation every Manifestation of God must needs vouchsafe
> to the peoples of His day a measure of divine guidance
> ampler than any which a preceding and less receptive age
> could have received or appreciated. (SHOGHI EFFENDI, *The
> World Order of Bahá'u'lláh* 102)

Less well known but perhaps equally significant, is the Bahá'í under-standing of progressive revelation within the history of each religion. Receptivity of the people to new spiritual insights grows as previously revealed teachings are digested and absorbed. Thus spiritual advancement is seen as an ongoing process within each religious community. To the extent that believers grasp and apply the fundamental teachings of their founding prophet, capacity for further learning is generated. Light begets light.

> This divinely purposed delay in the revelation of the basic
> laws of God for this age, and the subsequent gradual
> implementation of their provisions, illustrate the principle
> of progressive revelation which applies even within the
> ministry of each Prophet. (BAHÁ'U'LLÁH, *Kitáb-i-Aqdas,*
> Notes, p. 220)

In view of the central importance of progressive revelation, in both its macro and micro aspects, Bahá'í scholars have a special interest in documenting the interdependence of the world's religions. By identifying the specific threads of belief and practice as they persist and develop, scholars put flesh on the skeleton of progressive revelation. In addition, we often find an inter-fertility. It is not just the newer religions which borrow and adapt practices of the older, but also vigorous older religions adopting from latter revelations, as the value of new light becomes apparent. A unified vision of the interplay and interdependence of the world's spiritual heritage emerges.

The stepwise advancement of progressive revelation is seen to exist in all regions of the earth and encompass all spiritual traditions. In cases where we know only the current spiritual practice of an indigenous tribe and little of its history, it is assumed by faith that earlier developmental stages must have existed. The task of tracing the step-by-step progress is made easier when the spiritual history of a sequence of revelations is recorded in sacred books. This is precisely the case with the Abrahamic religions. Judaism, Christianity, Islam, coupled with the Bábí and Bahá'í Faiths, which constitute a millennia long series of discrete revelatory stages. The existence of the relevant sacred books, Torah, New Testament, Qur'án, Bábí and Bahá'í Writings, facilitate the work of any scholar who seeks to trace the specifics and mechanisms of progressive revelation.

This paper seeks to explore both the continuities and progressive unfoldments in daily prayer within the Abrahamic family of religions. Of course, this history is extensive and this paper cannot hope to trace the hundreds of forms that daily prayer has taken over the millennia. Nevertheless, certain interesting patterns emerge from a study of major trends. Worship has been transformed from its focus on communal sacrifices to a focus on individual communion with God through prayer. Daily prayer has now become, not only one of religion's essential practices, but the heart and soul of spirituality. The progressive elements of this transformation are seen blossoming within the sequence of divine revelations running from Moses to Bahá'u'lláh. These elements are traced in this paper from their roots in ancient Israel Temple sacrifice, through the development of synagogue and church liturgies of Judaism and Christianity, five- times daily prayer of Islam and the obligatory prayer of the Bahá'í Faith.

In general, we may think of spiritual progress growing out of the teachings of each new Prophet. Of special interest are those spiritual innovations that arise out of popular custom without a claim of divine mandate that are subsequently sanctified by a later Prophet.

To illustrate, there is no requirement for daily obligatory prayer in the Torah. Rather Jewish prayer practices developed over time at the Jerusalem Temple and were well established by popular custom within the Jewish Community before being sanctified by the revelations of Christ, Muhammad and Bahá'u'lláh.

Transformation: From Human to Animal Sacrifice

The history of the Abrahamic religions demonstrates patterns of worship with decreasing emphasis on communal worship orchestrated by a priesthood and increasing emphasis on individual worship. Prior to Abraham, child sacrifice was common in Near Eastern culture. The sites of ancient sacrificial cemeteries have been found from Amman, Jordan to Carthage in Tunisia. These cemeteries date from between the 15th century BCE and the 4th century BCE. (Some scholars claim that child sacrifice continued at Carthage into the second century CE but that conclusion is not universally accepted.) The burned skeletons of otherwise healthy children were buried in urns along with inscribed prayers and vows.

Child sacrifice was a deeply entrenched custom in Israel as well. Instances of child sacrifice persisted into the period of the Kings. Moabite King Mesa offered his son out of desperation while fighting a losing battle (2 Kings 3:27). Judahite Kings Ahaz and Manassah "do evil in the sight of the LORD" by burning their sons as offering (2 Kings 16:3; 21:6). A site of child sacrifice in the valley of Hinnom (Gehenna) was destroyed during Josiah's Reform in the late seventh century BCE (2 Kings 23:10; see http://www.usbible.com/Sacrifice/ sacrifice_israel.htm) The continuance of human sacrifices was a provocation to the Hebrew prophets. The prophet Micah decried those in his day who "give my firstborn for my transgression, the fruit of my body for the sin of my soul." (Micah 6:6–7)

In the Torah, Genesis 22, we find a poignant tale wherein an angel of the LORD puts an end to child sacrifice. It depicts Abraham traveling to Mount Moriah, binding his son, Isaac, and preparing to offer him in sacrifice in obedience to God's command. An angel intervened, halting the sacrifice. The story stirs compassion both for Isaac, as the intended victim, and for Abraham, as the one who must wield the sacrificial knife. The reader's sympathy for them prepares the way for the change in worship that follows. The old ways will give way to new ones. From then on offerings would be of animal only. As we read the story we emotionally align ourselves with Abraham and wonder how he will have the emotional strength to kill his own child. God says, "Take your son, your only son, the one you love and sacrifice him as a burnt offering." Not only is Isaac described as Abraham's son, but he is "the only son" and "the one you love." All this would make it incredibly difficult for Abraham to go through with the sacrifice. Later the emotional volume is raised even higher. As Abraham is climbing the mountain with his son, Isaac asks, "Where is the lamb for the burnt offering?" Isaac of course does not realize that he is the intended sacrificial victim.

Isaac is bound and laid out on the altar, but an angelic hand intervenes and halts the sacrifice. A sheep whose horns happen to be caught in a nearby bush, is offered up as a substitute. Thereafter those who worshipped in the Abrahamic tradition would no longer follow the long standing practice of sacrificing first born children. The reform was later encoded in the Torah prohibiting all human sacrifice (Leviticus 18:21; 20:2–5).

Can the ban on human sacrifice aptly be termed "progressive revelation?" Some may object claiming that God never commanded the sacrifice of children. Indeed we have no ancient record of any such pre-Abrahamic command. Yet progressive revelation need not be limited to abrogation of one divine law by another. Revelation of new laws that change common practices serves the same purpose. Clearly the ban on human sacrifice can rightly be called "progress" as it raised the value of human life and transformed belief regarding what God required from His worshippers. This new vision of God was less harshly demanding, more compassionate.

Further this ban was the first in a chain of reforms that would span multiple revelations. Soon thereafter the first foreshadows of the end of the sacrificial cult appeared.

> Does the LORD delight in sacrifice and burnt offering rather than obeying the voice of the LORD? Behold to obey is better than to sacrifice, to heed is better than the fat of rams. [1 Samuel 15:22)

Although further centuries would be required, the end of the sacrificial cult was destined to follow.

Transformation: From Sacrifice to Prayer

From Abraham's time through the Exodus, obligatory worship revolved primarily around cultic worship with animal sacrifices on special occasions presided over by holy men, such as priests or family patriarchs. Prayer was largely spontaneous. We find no information regarding systematic daily worship, either prayer or sacrifice during the patriarchal age. Prayer at that time appears to have been on an "as needed" basis and consisted primarily of petitions in times of need. (Genesis 20:7) Only with the Torah, and the establishment of the Tabernacle along with a professional priesthood, do we find regulations regarding obligatory daily worship of any kind.

> Now this is what you shall offer on the altar: two lambs of the first year, day by day constantly. One lamb you shall offer in the morning, and the other lamb you shall offer at twilight . . . And you shall offer it with grain offering and drink offering . . . for a sweet aroma, an offering made by fire to the LORD. This shall be a continual burnt offering throughout your generations at the door of the tabernacle of meeting before the LORD . . . (Exodus 29:38–42)

> And you shall make an altar to burn incense on . . . Aaron
> shall burn on it sweet incense every morning when he tends
> the lamps. And when Aaron lights the lamps at twilight, he
> shall burn incense upon it, a perpetual incense before the
> LORD throughout your generations. (Exodus 30:1, 7–8)

Surprisingly, however, the instructions to the priests contain no
mention of prayers to be offered in conjunction with the daily burnt
offerings. Prayer continued to be primarily associated with petitions
for aid (Numbers 21:7) or special occasion blessings (Leviticus 9:22;
Numbers 6:24–26). Odd as it may seem to us, in view of our con-
temporary association of worship and prayer, there apparently were
no formalized daily prayers in the time of either Abraham or Moses.
If regular prayers of praise or thanksgiving were used, we have no
record of them. The earliest mention of daily pray in the Biblical
record appears around the time of the establishment of the Israelite
monarchy under Kings David and Solomon.

The enlargement of the role of prayer was coupled with an
expanded view of the purpose of prayer. Prayer was no longer limited to petitions for aid which tend to arise spontaneously in response
to specific hurtful or potentially hurtful situations. In contrast, daily
prayers were used day in and day out, during good times and bad.
Prayer became a vehicle for a wider variety of spiritual expressions
including praise, thanksgiving and lamentation.

The book of Psalms contains 150 sacred songs, many ascribed
to David. Expressions such as "Give thanks unto the LORD, for He
is Good" (136:1), "Every day I will bless you" (145:2) and "Hallelujah, Praise ye God" (150:6) indicate that praise and thanksgiving
were an integral part of tabernacle and temple worship. The existence of a collection of songs indicates some sort of regular use. Yet
the Psalter contains little explicit indication of how or when these
sacred songs were sung. One notable exception is Psalm 92, which
reads in part:

A Psalm. A Song for the Sabbath Day. It is good to give
thanks to the LORD,
And to sing praises to Your name, O Most High; To
declare Your loving kindness in the morning, And Your
faithfulness every night,
On an instrument of ten strings, On the lute and on the
harp,
With harmonious sounds. (Psalm 92:1–3)

The paradox here is that despite the pledge of daily praise, we find
the superscription associates the psalm with the Sabbath rather than
daily worship. Even though the words of the song refer to daily
praise, we do not know whether there was any kind of a daily worship service at the tabernacle, or if such existed what the contents of
the service might have been. We know even less about the prayer life
of average Israelites. Did they have daily or special occasion prayers?
Were the psalms known and used by common people in the course
of their everyday lives? We simply do not know. We do know, however, that if such existed, it was not mandatory or encoded in sacred
literature. Worship during that early period still revolved primarily
around sacrifices.

In his prayer dedicating the Jerusalem Temple, it is significant
that King Solomon refers to the Temple as "a house of prayer" rather
than a house of sacrifice. This phrase broke new ground, helping
to create a new prayer emphasis. He pleaded, "May You hear the
supplication of . . . Your people Israel, when they pray towards this
place . . . (also) the foreigner when he comes and prays toward this
Temple . . . " (1 Kings 8:30, 43). "When anyone sins," "when Israel
is defeated," "when there is famine in the land" (1 Kings 8:22:53) the
people were directed to pray towards the new Temple. The presence
of God resided in the Holy of Holies of the Temple as represented by
the miraculous Shekinah Light that resided above the outstretched
cherub's wings above the Ark of the Covenant. Within the Ark were

the Tablets of Moses containing the Ten Commandments. Thus, Solomon's Temple with its Shekinah Light was a suitable magnet for supplication and petition. However, even in connection with Solomon's House of Prayer, we find no descriptions of daily prayer.

Some verses in the Psalms and Prophets seem on first reading to refer to daily prayer routines. These verses were later used anachronistically as evidence of the antiquity of the practice. However, rather than being daily prayer as we now conceive it, offered every day of the year, good times and bad, these references on close reading can be seen as describing relatively short periods of intense prayer during times of trouble. In the Psalms, we find David praying for relief three times a day. "As for me, I will call upon God; and the LORD shall save me. Evening, and morning, and at noon, will I pray, and cry aloud; and he shall hear my voice" (55:17). The context shows that David had been betrayed by an unnamed friend and was praying for God's protection against this new enemy (vv, 18;21). Daniel is also described praying three times a day in response to trouble, a royal prohibition against worshipping the God of Israel. (Daniel 6:10). Prayer was still for special occasions, medicine to be administered on an 'as needed' basis.

A significant innovation in the role of prayer was expressed in the Psalms of David and became even more fully developed in the writings of Jeremiah. A new intimacy arose, establishing a different sort of relationship. Previously prayer had been formal and emotionally distant as implied in the imagery of the supplicant humbly entering a royal court in order to petition the King. Now, we see something more than the vertical standing of sovereign versus subject. David poured out his heart to God in prayer, shared his inner life and inmost feelings, expressed negative emotions, lamentations, fears, doubts, as well as joy and exhilaration.

My God, My God, why have you forsaken me? (Psalm 22:1)

O LORD, do not rebuke me in your anger, nor chasten me in your hot displeasure. Have mercy on my O LORD, for I am weak. O LORD, heal me for my bones are troubled. (Psalm 6:1–2)

I will praise you O LORD, with my whole heart. I will tell of your marvelous works. I will be glad and rejoice in You. (Psalm 9:1–2)

Jeremiah took this intimacy a step further. After the destruction of Jerusalem and the First Temple, he wrote a series of poems called Lamentations, describing the dejected state of the Jewish nation. He poured out his heart in sorrow without making request for relief. His sole interest was for God to see him and to recognize his pain of heart. "O LORD, behold my affliction . . . " (Lamentations 1:9). "See O LORD, for I am in distress" (1:20). The purpose of these prayers was neither praise nor petition, but open self-expression. Jeremiah's freeness of speech allowed him to go so far as to express disappointment with God. "You fooled me, O God, so that I was fooled." (20:7) For this reason, Wellhausen called Jeremiah, "the father of true prayer . . . his book contains . . . confessions of personal troubles and desperate struggles." (Idelsohn, 15) God was now more than the Almighty Sovereign Creator of Heaven and Earth. He had also become "the Friend."

The Babylonian Exile brought new challenges to worshippers of Yahweh, the God of Israel, They were deprived of their Temple and the accompanying sacrificial rites. Prayer thus took on greater and greater importance. Even after the return to Zion and the rebuilding of the Temple, many Jews remained in Babylon and shortly thereafter spread even further afield. By the third century BCE, significant Jewish populations could be found throughout the Hellenized Middle East. Synagogues, as a center of Jewish spiritual life arose during the Second Temple period as a practical adaptation to life in the Diaspora. Travel to the Temple entailed a difficult and expensive journey from Alexandria, Rome or Babylon. Large numbers did manage to get to the annual pilgrimage festivals, Passover, Pentecost and Succoth, but only the most affluent could afford to attend three times each year. Furthermore, Temple worship took place amidst the congregated throng and allowed little place for study, discussion of the Holy texts or private meditation. The synagogue developed as a supplement to Temple worship, a place for Torah reading and Sabbath prayer.

As a relatively late development, synagogues are not mentioned in the Hebrew Bible. The earliest appeared during the third century BCE in lower Egypt and slowly spread around the Mediterranean. (see Second Temple Synagogues, http://www.pohick.org/sts/) Remains of early synagogues in Europe have been found in Delos, Greece, and Ostia, Italy. The spiritual advantages of weekly Sabbath gatherings for study and prayer invigorated Jewish communities in the Diaspora. Once these advantages were recognized, synagogues began to appear in the Holy Land around the first century BCE as witnessed by ruins discovered at Gamala and Capernaum (Galilee region), Masada, and eventually reaching even to Jerusalem in the shadow of the Temple Mount by the mid-first century CE.

The earliest synagogue in Judea has been unearthed at Qumran, the sectarian Jewish community in the Judean Desert where the Dead Sea Scrolls were found. This group despised the corrupt Jerusalem priesthood and separated themselves to a life of isolation in the desert. They redefined the Temple as their holy community made up of living stones (Isaiah 54:11) and extended priestly rituals of purity to all community members. In obedience to the Laws regarding Temple rites, they bathed several times daily as the priests did, and offered the sweet fragrances of prayer, the burnt offerings of the lips (Hosea 14:2), twice daily as a substitute for the evening and morning sacrifices as prescribed in the Torah for the Temple. At Qumran, prayer was not just for the priests, nor was it limited to festival days or times of need. Rather prayer was systematized and became daily practice for the entire community. As far as we know, this is the first instance of obligatory daily prayer that is now central to Judaism, Christianity, Islam and the Bahá'í Faith.

According to the beliefs of the Qumran community, God had abandoned the Holy of Holies of the Temple and now resided among them. The estrangement from the Temple cult may have given the synagogue its initial boost in the Holy Land, but its growth encompassed both establishment and antiestablishment Jews. A Greek inscription at the site of the Jerusalem synagogue declared, "Theodotus, (son) of Vettenus, priest . . . built the synagogue for the reading of the law and the teaching of the commandments." Priests also saw value in the synagogue as a supplement to Temple worship, primarily as a library to allow public access to the sacred scrolls. It was a place for reading and studying Torah. But while the Temple stood, prayer was not yet a focus of synagogue activity.

After the destruction of the Jerusalem Temple by the Romans in 70 CE, Judaism underwent a major transformation. The cessation of the Temple cult brought an end to the leadership role of the priesthood within the Jewish community.

> As their world began to urbanize, the rabbis offered a bold new concept of a Judaism which was no longer dependant on the agricultural environment . . . Rites of sacrifice lost their raison d'être . . . In the eyes of most Jews, sacrifices could only be offered at the centralized cultic site in Jerusalem. Consequently, Titus' destruction of the Temple meant that the various daily, weekly and monthly sacrifices as well as the annual festivals could no longer take place. (http://www.pohick.org/sts/Intrononotes.html)

First century Rabbis met at the Council of Yavneh to establish the canon of the Tanakh and establish schools for the study of those sacred texts. The Talmud grew out of their deliberations. Prayer came to fill the void left by the end of the sacrificial cult and pilgrimage festivals. A systematic liturgy emerged with a specific order of prayers recited at specific times of the day.

Daily Prayer in Judaism

The earliest daily obligatory prayers in Judaism arose after the destruction of the Second Temple. Jews would hold daily gatherings, called minyans, in the synagogue up to three times a day. The Talmud specifies that at the times when the morning and evening sacrifices had been offered, the portions of the law that govern the sacrifices should be recited. "your children shall study the law concerning sacrifices and I (God) will consider it as though they had actually offered them and I will forgive their sins." (b. Meg. 31b)

In post-Biblical practice, the Shema is the core expression of Jewish faith, declaring the Oneness of God. "Sh'ma, Israel, Adonai Elohenu, Adonai Echad" which translated means "Hear O Israel, the LORD our God, the Lord is One" (Deuteronomy 6:4), the Shema came to be recited twice a day. Whether there was originally a linkage to the morning and evening Temple sacrifices is unknown. Repetition of the Shema is not a Torah Law, but rather a custom that developed long after Moses. Although, the text itself is found in the Hebrew Bible, which was the Book of that Age, there are no instructions within the text stating that the verse should be recited.

Tradition holds that public recitation of the Shema originated in the days of the Second Temple, no later than the first century CE. Recitation of the Shema entailed not just the famous verse affirming the oneness of God (Deuteronomy 6:4) but included related passages from the Torah as follows: Deuteronomy 6:4-9 which speaks of the unity and love of God, Deuteronomy 11:13-21 which rehearses the results of obedience and disobedience to divine Torah and sets out the necessity of teaching Torah to children, and Numbers 15:37-41 which reiterates the need for obedience to Torah and sets out ordinances related to clothing which serve as symbols of God's covenant with Israel.

Another ancient prayer found in synagogue liturgy is called the Amidah. Based on the example of King David, it is a blessing repeated morning, noon and night (Psalms 55:17–18), three times a day. The Amidah is a prayer that is recited in a standing position from which its name is derived. It contains eighteen benedictions and acknowledges the faith of the forefathers of the Israelite nation. The form of the Amidah was at first somewhat flexible, with only the text of the first and last three benedictions definitely fixed. Spontaneous expressions and petitions were incorporated into the intermediary benedictions. Later the entire text of the eighteen benedictions was solidified. English translations of both the Shema and Amidah are found in Appendix A.

The recitation of these and other prayers was accompanied by the use of tefillin or phylacteries. Small leather cases containing written prayers and other holy words were tied onto the head and hands of the worshipper with long straps. The practice is based on a literal interpretation of the Biblical injunction:

> And these words, which I command thee this day, shall be upon thy heart ... And thou shalt bind them for a sign upon thy hand, and they shall be for frontlets between thine eyes. (Devarim / Deuteronomy 6:6–8)

Ablutions were also part of Jewish daily prayer customs. According to the Talmud, Berachot 14b-15a, hands were to be washed before adorning tefillin or reciting either the Shema or the Amidah prayer.It appears that originally these prayers were said privately but over time the practice developed of congregating morning, noon and night for services. Each service includes the recitation of the Shema. Only the evening and morning services include the Amidah. Orthodox "minyans" or daily prayer services have followed the same basic pattern with little variation from at least the fourth century CE until the present.

As synagogue architecture developed in later centuries, that divine presence was enshrined in an ark at the front of the synagogue containing the Torah scrolls in remembrance of the Ark of the Covenant and the Holy Tablets of the Jerusalem Temple. An Eternal Light, representing the Temple's Shekinah, was suspended over the Ark. Evening and morning animal offerings were transformed into prayers. Priests were no longer needed. A new class of professional religious leaders arose to take their place. Rabbis were scholars, learned in the Holy Books. The new emphasis was on recitation and study of the sacred texts. Although conceived of as only a temporary substitute for the destroyed temple, the synagogue became the center of religious life, the place where the presence of God was seen to reside.

Despite the accommodation to life in the Diaspora, an orientation to the Holy Land and the site of the destroyed Temple was ever present. The irreplaceable sanctity of the Holy City was, according to both the Mishnah and Gemarah, memorialized by the direction one faced while praying.

> If one is standing outside the country, one should direct one's heart to the Land of Israel. If one stands in the Land of Israel, one should direct one's heart towards Jerusalem. If one is standing in Jerusalem, one should direct one's heart towards the Temple. If one is standing in the Temple, one should direct one's heart towards the Holy of Holies. Consequently, if one is in the East, one should turn his face toward the West; if in the West, one should turn towards the East; if in the South, one should turn towards the North; if in the North, one should turn towards the South. In this way, all Israel will be directing their hearts towards one place. (Talmud Berakhot 30a)

The Emerging Christian Liturgy

Christianity was built upon the foundation of Moses and the Hebrew prophets. The first Christians were Jews who continued to attend local synagogue services. In some areas, Christians were forced to separate themselves due to being branded heretics and kicked out of the synagogue. In other places, Christians and Jews continued to pray together for centuries. There are reports of a fifth century Byzantine Bishop chastising Christian groups for failing to separate from the synagogue.

Long periods of joint worship, however, were the exception rather than the rule. Twenty years after the death of Christ, separate Christian Churches were well established in many large cities in Palestine, Asia Minor (now Turkey) and Greece. Yet, except for a few Apostolic Letters, they had no sacred text of their own on which to base their prayer services. The formation of the New Testament did not begin until decades after the death of Christ. Thus, the young Church was forced to borrow heavily from the text and traditions of Judaism. During those early years, Christians met in small groups in private homes, just as Jews did when communities lacked the resources to have their own synagogue. Congregational worship was weekly, either on the Sabbath or on the first day of the week. The structure was open, flexible and participatory. Anyone in attendance could stand up and spontaneously contribute.

> When ye come together (for worship) one brings a psalm, another a teaching, another a tongue, another a revelation, another an interpretation. Let all things be done to edify. (1 Corinthians 14:26)

At that early stage, there was no established liturgy, but rather considerable latitude to shape the service according to the expectations, talents and needs of each particular Church community. Church services were modeled after the synagogue and therefore highlighted reading of the Hebrew Bible, the singing of psalms and teachings (sermons). However, early Church services were distinguished from synagogue services by the presence of miraculous gifts of the spirit such as tongues, revelations and interpretations thereof. Over time, readings from the Gospels were gradually added along with the recitation of formalized Christian prayers and creeds. However, reading from the Old Testament and the singing of Psalms has ever remained an integral part of Christian worship.

Christian Daily Prayer

One of the most significant innovations of the Christian Revelation was a progressive view of animal sacrifice. While acknowledging the divine origin of the Mosaic Law and the sacrificial rites found in the Torah, they were viewed as part of the old Covenant that had been replaced by the New. While Judaism kept the hope of the restoration of the sacrificial cults alive while adapting to the loss of the Second Temple, Christians viewed the end of the cult as permanent. There would no longer be any need for the Jerusalem Temple, altars of burnt offering, or sacrifices of bulls, goats or sheep.

The death of Christ on the cross was seen as a superior sacrifice with the power to cleanse humanity once for all time. Temple rites were reinterpreted; Christ as High Priest offering the value of His Life in a heavenly, rather than earthly, Temple. (Hebrews 9:24–26)

The loss of sacrifice as a means of approach to the divine left a vacuum that prayer filled. Prayer replaced the offerings of incense and the smoke of burnt offerings ascending to God. Christians were to immerse themselves in prayer and to "pray incessantly" (Romans 12:12).

The Didache, also known as the Teachings of the Twelve Apostles, is a post-Biblical Christian work generally dated circa 115 CE. In it we find the earlier known set format for daily Christian prayer. It instructs believers to recite the Lord's Prayer three times each day.

Neither pray ye as the hypocrites, but as the Lord hath commanded in his gospel so pray ye: 'Our Father in heaven, hallowed be thy name. Thy kingdom come. Thy will be done as in heaven so on earth. Give us this day our daily bread. And forgive us our debt, as we also forgive our debtors. And lead us not into temptation, but deliver us from the evil: for thine is the power, and the glory, for ever.' Thrice a day pray ye in this fashion. (Didache: 8:2–3)

It is unclear how widespread the thrice daily recitation of the Lord's Prayer was among early Christians, since the authenticity of Didache was not universally accepted. Some Christian communities claimed it to be genuine Apostolic Instruction originating in the Jerusalem Council of 50 CE. Clement of Alexandria (second century) cites it once as Scripture, but no one else among the Church Fathers makes any reference to it before the time of Eusebius (fourth century). Eusebius emphatically places it among books that were not to be included in the New Testament canon. Yet apparently Didache enjoyed a wide circulation and was accepted by at least a portion of the Church as a book worthy to be read in Church services. Athanasius reports that it was still used for catechetical instruction in the late fourth century. Thus it seems likely that a considerable number of Christians would have followed its prescription for saying the Lord's Prayer three times in a day.

Eucharist and Catholic Mass

Another Christian innovation was communion or the Eucharist. Christ had transformed the Jewish Passover into a memorial of His sacrificial death. The bread and wine of the Passover meal became the sacraments of his Memorial from which, over time, the liturgy Catholic Sacrifice of the Mass developed. For some time the Eucharistic Service was fluid and variable.

All ceremonial evolves gradually out of certain obvious actions done at first with no idea of ritual, but simply because they had to be done for convenience. The bread and wine were brought to the altar when they were wanted, the lessons were read from a place where they could best be heard, hands were washed because they were soiled. Out of these obvious actions ceremony developed . . .

But we find much more than this essential nucleus in use in every Church from the first century. The Eucharist was always celebrated at the end of a service of lessons, psalms, prayers, and preaching, which was itself merely a continuation of the service of the synagogue. So we have everywhere this double function; first, a synagogue service Christianized, in which the holy books were read, psalms were sung, prayers said by the bishop in the name of all (the people answering "Amen" in Hebrew, as had their Jewish forefathers), and homilies, explanations of what had been read, were made by the bishop or priests, just as they had been made in the synagogues by the learned men and elders (e. g., Luke, iv, 16-27). This is what was known afterwards as the Liturgy of the Catechumens. Then followed the Eucharist . . .

. . . bread and wine are brought to the celebrant in vessels (a plate and a cup); he puts them on a table—the altar; standing before it in the natural attitude of prayer he takes them in his hands, gives thanks, as our Lord had done, says again the words of institution, breaks the Bread and gives the consecrated Bread and Wine to the people in communion . . . (http://www.newadvent.org/cathen/09306a.html)

The text of the Didache provided instructions on how the Eucharist was to be celebrated. Parameters are set such as specific prayers to bless the bread and wine before communion and a specific prayer to follow it. This latter prayer pleads for the unity of the Church by creating an interesting interpretive link between the bread of the last supper and the miracle of the multiplication of loaves.

> As this broken bread was scattered upon the mountains and being gathered together became one, so may Thy Church be gathered together from the ends of the earth into Thy kingdom; for Thine is the glory and the power through Jesus Christ for ever and ever. (http://earlychristianwritings.com/text/didache-lightfoot.html)

The Didache speaks to Christians and refers to the Eucharist as "your sacrifice." More was involved than a memorial of Christ's sacrificial death long past. The offering was brought into the present. The participants could share in and experience of the vital moment of salvation. Here we have one of the earliest hints of Transubstantiation, the doctrine that is the basis for the Catholic Sacrifice of the Mass.

Among the writings of the Apostolic Fathers, Justin Martyr (c. 101–150 CE) gives further evidence as to the identification of the Last Supper with a sacrificial offering. ". . . we have been taught that the food which is blessed by the prayer of His word, and from which our blood and flesh by transmutation are nourished, is the flesh and blood of that Jesus who was made flesh" (First Apology, 1, 62). Transmutation, or transubstantiation as it was later called, is the doctrine that the bread and wine of the celebration of the Last Supper are miraculously changed during the service into the actual flesh and blood of Christ, thus bringing the sacrifice of the cross into the spiritual reality of the celebration.

As to when and how often the Eucharist was celebrated, many scholars link descriptions of Sunday Service liturgy with the descriptions of the Eucharist in both Didache and Justin Martyr's Apology. But a careful reading leaves that link in doubt. Both texts contain detailed descriptions of weekly services that omit clear reference to the Eucharist, which is previously described in considerable detail. That separation seems strange if the Eucharist and Sunday Service had already been united at the early date. Nevertheless, sometime during the second century the Eucharist became a weekly observance. By the third century, Cyprian (c. 200–258) argued that the Eucharist was to be celebrated daily on the basis of Christ's prayer, "Give us this day our daily bread."

The liturgy of the Mass incorporates the use of various body positions: kneeling, sitting and standing.

Liturgy of the Hours

The Liturgy of the Hours constitutes a series of prayers that were used in Catholic monasteries from ancient times. In its late and complete form, prayer services were held seven times during the day (Psalms 119:164) and once at midnight (Acts 16:25). Each service bore a Latin name, several of which corresponded to the Roman custom of numbering the hours of the day starting from dawn. The schedule may have looked like this:

> Lauds—Dawn
> Prime—One hour after dawn or approximately 7 AM
> Terce—Three hours after dawn, c. 9 AM
> Sext—Six hours after dawn, c. Noon
> None—Nine hours after dawn, c. 3 PM
> Vespers—c. 5 PM
> Compline—7 PM
> Matins—Midnight

The monks would sleep in the early evening after Compline, rise at midnight for the Matins and then return to bed thereafter.

This intricate system of prayer did not spring into existence fully formed. The Catholic Encyclopedia expresses the view that the Liturgy of the Hours originally consisted of three daily services, Terce, Sext and None. The writings of the Ante-Nicean Fathers instruct all Christians to pray at these hours, but give no indication of whether private prayer or congregational prayer was intended.

> Clement of Alexandria and likewise Tertullian, as early as the end of the second century, expressly mention the hours of Terce, Sext, and None, as specially set apart for prayer (Clement, "Strom.," VII, VII, in P.G., IX, 455-8). Tertullian says explicitly that we must always pray, and that there is no time prescribed for prayer; he adds, nevertheless, these significant words: "As regards the time, there should be no lax observation of certain hours—I mean of those common hours which have long marked the divisions of the day, the third, the sixth, and the ninth, and which we may observe in Scripture to be more solemn than the rest" ("De Oratione," xxiii, xxv, in P.L., I, 1191–3). (*Catholic Encyclopedia*, Electronic Version, http://www.newadvent. org/cathen/none.html)

In stages, the number of times a day specified for formal prayer increased. Practicality limited observance to monasteries as working people could not comply with so rigorous a prayer schedule. By the end of the fourth century, the hours of Vigils (Matins), Lauds and Vespers had been added. The full repertoire of eight services was in place by the end of the fifth century. The selection of these hours was based on certain times that Peter and other apostles are reported to have prayed. Rather than obedience to a specific injunction, the multitude of services is perhaps best understood as an attempt to institutionalize the apostolic mandate to "pray incessantly."

Modern Catholic, Orthodox and Protestant Liturgies

Over the centuries, Church liturgies tended to grow more and more structured. Nevertheless, tremendous variety can be found from one denomination to the next. Virtually all incorporate the singing of psalms (or hymns), a sermon (or teaching) and the Eucharist (or Holy Communion). Many also include recitation of the Lord's Prayer.

Catholic and Orthodox Services are highly scripted. For example the Greek Orthodox Service as found in the Divine Liturgy of St. John Chrysostomos (http://www.ocf.org/OrthodoxPage/liturgy/ liturgy.html) consists largely of responsive readings coupled with recited creeds and prayers. Protestant Services vary widely from well developed structure found in Lutheran and Anglican Churches to the relative spontaneity of the Baptist and Pentecostal Churches.

Christian Innovations

Judaism began with an orientation to the sacred space of the tabernacle / temple and only later adopted the scattered locations of the synagogue as a proxy. Christianity however began with distributed sacred space, space that was sanctified simply by assembling. "For where two or three are gathered together in my name, there am I in the midst of them." (Matthew 18:20) The sacred geography of the past would be abandoned. "The hour cometh, when ye shall neither in this mountain, nor yet at Jerusalem, worship the Father." (John 4:21) The idealized vision of Christian worship found in the Revelation of St. John portrays a Christian community oriented to a New Jerusalem a spiritual city built on the foundation of the Twelve Apostles with Christ as the foundation cornerstone.

> And he carried me away in the spirit to a great and high mountain, and shewed me that great city, the holy Jerusalem, descending out of heaven from God . . . And I saw no

temple therein: for the Lord God Almighty and the Lamb
are the temple of it. And the city had no need of the sun,
neither of the moon, to shine in it: for the glory of God
did lighten it, and the Lamb is the light thereof. And the
nations of them which are saved shall walk in the light
of it: and the kings of the earth do bring their glory and
honour into it. (Revelation 21:10, 22–24)

In this vision, Jerusalem retains its Holy status, as it did within
Judaism, but the city was to be Temple-less. God and Christ would
serve the orienting function that the physical Temple had previously
served. Under Byzantine rule, Jerusalem was a center of Christian
Life. Churches were constructed at the sites related to the life and
death of "the LORD" but the Temple Mount was intentionally left in
ruins. The entire City was sacred, but no specific place within the City
was identified with the presence of God.

Interestingly both Judaism and early Christianity made the
transition from Temple oriented to congregation oriented worship
at about the same time during the first century C.E. Jews view this
transition as temporary and continued to anticipate the restoration of
the sacrificial cult. In contrast, Christianity was born at the tail end of
the Second Temple period and viewed the destruction of the Temple
as a sign of that a new covenant had replaced the old Law of Moses.
Nevertheless, both groups built upon the rituals of animal sacrifices
and transformed them into symbolic acts. The breaking of bread, the
drinking of wine and most prominently, offerings of incessant prayer
took the place of the former rites.

Christ, like David and Jeremiah, poured out His personal lamentations to God in prayer at critical times. Prior to His arrest in the
Garden of Gethsemane the Gospels report Christ's words, "My soul is
deeply grieved even unto death . . . Father let this cup pass from me."
(Matthew 26:38–39) On the cross, Christ's lament took up David's
anguished cry from the Psalm, "God, why have you forsaken me?"
(Matthew 27:46) Perhaps one of the most revolutionary innovations

by some Protestant groups is the rejection of the recitation of written prayers. Prayers are said in one's own words. For some denominations, such as the Church of Christ and Jehovah's Witnesses, the prohibition extends even to reciting the Lord's Prayer. Although this prayer is the oldest documented portion of the Church liturgy, its repetition is not mandated in the text of the New Testament. Opponents of 'rote prayer' will point out that in the Gospel text, in the verses just prior to the Lord's Prayer, Jesus warns his disciples against repetitive prayer.

> When ye pray, use not vain repetitions, as the heathen do: for they think that they shall be heard for their much speaking. Be not ye therefore like unto them: for your Father knoweth what things ye have need of, before ye ask him. After this manner therefore pray ye: Our Father which art in heaven, Hallowed be thy name. (Matthew 6:7–9)

This command has been interpreted as prohibiting the verbatim repletion of any kind. The result is a wholesale dismissal of liturgy. Services in these churches tend to enlarge the teaching / sermon portion of the service.

Within this branch of Protestantism, prayer is seen as a vehicle for establishing a "personal relationship with God." Spontaneous, unscripted prayers uttered in one's own words, serves to create an intimate link with the Divine. Nevertheless, distinct prayer patterns persist even in these 'anti-rote' churches. The use of psalms and hymns (often prayers set to music) is common to virtually all Christian denominations.

Islam

Daily prayer, referred to in Arabic as al-Salat, is one of the founding principles of Islam. Muhammad established specific times of the day and specific regulation for prayer. The Qur'án does not portray al-Salat as an Islamic innovation but rather traces its origin back to the Patriarchal Age. Abraham, Isaac, Jacob (21:73), Ishmael (19:55), Moses (20:14) and Jesus (19:31) are all said to have practiced regular prayer. Subsequent generations failed to preserve their heritage and ancient prayer practices needed to be reestablished by Muhammad .

> These are some of the prophets whom God blessed. They were chosen from among the descendants of Adam, and the descendants of those whom we carried with Noah, and the descendants of Abraham and Israel, and from among those whom we guided and selected. When the revelations of the Most Gracious are recited to them, they fall prostrate, weeping. After them, He substituted generations who lost the contact prayers (Salat) and pursued their lusts . . . (Qur'án 19:58–59)

Current practice is highly structured including specific hours of prayer five times a day. A series of formalized prayers called a raka' is used. The cycle is repeated a specified number of times at each designated hours. For example, the morning prayers, called Salat-ul- Fajr, consist of two cycles while the noon prayers, Salat-ul-Zuhr, consist of four.

Key elements of each cycle proclaim the greatness and oneness as embodied in the phrases, Alláh'u'Akbar (God is Great) and La ilaha illalláh (There is no God but God). In contrast to informal prayers, which can be said at any time of the day or night, al-Salat customs are specified for the designated hours. There is almost universal conformity throughout the Muslim world on the following prayer procedure, although some local variants do exist.

1. Ablutions or ritual washing, prior to prayer.
2. Pray facing the Qiblih at Mecca.
3. Verbatim recitation of specified prayers including portions of Qur'án,

4. Use of specific prayer postures such as bowing, kneeling and standing at specific points in the prayer,
5. Performed five times each day at specified hours.

Ritual cleansing is an important part of Islamic prayer practice. Mosques often contain facilities for ablutions. Parts of the body are washed in a specific order according to a specified procedure. For example, one is to take water in the palm of the right hand and wash the face top to bottom, from forehead to chin. This outward physical preparation is to be accompanied by an inner preparation for the heart's connection with the divine. One then faces Mecca and recites a series of short prayers in praise of God. Each is said from a specified position: standing, kneeling or bowing.

Qur'ánic Origins of Traditional Prayer Practices

The general belief among Muslims is that all of the prayer practices associated with al-Salat go back at least to the time of Muhammad . (Some claim they go back to Abraham.) God is said to have revealed these details to Muhammad during the Prophet's night journey (Isra' and Mi'raj). In fact, while certain features of Salat are clearly set forth in the Qur'án, such as times of day and the direction to face, other specifics such as the text of the prayers to be used, the details of ablutions, the specific positions to go with each part of the text or the number of cycles (raka') to say at each hour, are not recorded in the Qur'án. Rather they derive from secondary sources (Hadith) and later traditions.

Chapter 4 of the Qur'án is one of its oldest sections. It deals with a early period in the career of Muhammad, just after the Hegira, when He resided in Medina. The text shows that even in that period daily prayer routines had already been established. "Prayer indeed has been enjoined upon the believers at fixed times." (4:103) They were performed publicly and accompanied by prostrations (4:102). In times of danger or battle, prayers could be shortened (4:101). This exemption indicates that already in the Medina period, Muhammad 's followers had formalized daily prayers of specified length, which then could be shortened under exceptional circumstances.

The five times for Al-Salat are set at dawn, noon, mid-afternoon, sunset and night (before retiring). Most Islamic authorities recognize the authority for these five distinct hours of prayer as originating in the Qur'án:

- Dawn—"Establish regular prayers . . . the morning prayer" (17:78); "at the retreat of the stars" (52:49); "before the rising of the sun" (20:130) "at the two ends of the day [i.e. morning and evening]" (11:114).

- Noon—"(Say) Glory be to Alláh . . . when the day begins to decline." (30:18)

- Afternoon (or before sunset)—"Keep up prayer at the ends of the day [understood as beginning and end of daylight]" (11:114); "in the late afternoon" (30:18)

- Sunset (after sundown)—"Keep up prayer . . . in the first hours of the night." (11:114)

- Night—(before going to bed)- "So (give) glory to God, when ye reach eventide and when ye rise in the morning." (30:17)

Some scholars (mostly non-Islamic) identify only three times of prayer in these verses, dawn, sunset and nighttime. (See Judaism in Islam by Abraham Katsh, p. xv) They would understand "when the day begins to decline" as signifying the hour before sunset rather than noon and they would understand "in the first hours of the night" as equivalent to bedtime. Thus the second and third salats would be collapsed, likewise the fourth and fifth. If true, separation into 5 prayer times would be understood as a later development.

Interestingly, some Muslims also see evidence for three rather than five daily prayers based upon the text of Qur'án 11:114 which reads, "And establish regular prayers at the two ends of the day and at the approaches of the night."

> The two afternoon prayers and the two after sunset prayers, which are spoken of together, may . . . be said together. (Notes to Maulana Muhammad Ali's translation of the Qur'án)

> As for the Establishing of our PRAYERS, Alláh has mentioned only THREE TIMES in the Qur'án. (http://www.mostmerciful.com/realities-of-our-daily-prayers-part--three-conclusion.htm [sic; URL correct])

When we compare ancient Jewish and Islamic prayer practice, some interesting parallels emerge. The Hebrew Bible describes the prayers of Daniel in terms that resemble al-Salat in several particulars. We read, ". . . he went into his house; and his windows being open in his chamber toward Jerusalem, he kneeled upon his knees three times a day and prayed, and gave thanks before his God . . ." (Daniel 6:10). Here Daniel (a) faces the Holy City, (b) assumes a kneeling posture, (c) prays three times a day.

If the proposals regarding an original three times prayer in Islam is accurate, it would bring early Islamic practice into closer conformity with Jewish and Christian practice. Disputes with Jews and Christians, during and after Muhammad's lifetime, may well have lead to a variety of reforms within Islam as the new religion sought to establish its own independent identity. We know from the Qur'án itself that the direction of prayer, the Qiblih, had been moved from Jerusalem to Mecca for precisely this reason.

Striking similarities exist between the Jewish Shema and the Islamic Shahadah. Both are fundamental confessions of monotheism.

The kernel of the Shema is "Hear O Israel, the LORD thy God, the LORD is one." The Shahadah similarly asserts, "There is no God but Allāh. (la ilaha illa 'llāhu)" The Shahadah also parallels other Biblical passages such as, "There is no God but the LORD." (Psalms 18:31) Both Jewish and Islamic daily prayers invoke the name of God and offer superlative praise, both acknowledge their respective founders, Moses and Muhammad, (Compare Tashahhud lines 3-6 with Amidah line 2) and both encourage loyalty to God's law. (Compare Qira'ah lines 7–9 with portion of Shema form Numbers 15:40) Al-Salat is always said in Arabic, regardless of the native language of the believer, as Jewish prayers are always offered in Hebrew.

Animal Sacrifice in Islam

The feast of Eid al-Adha is celebrated on the 10th day of the month of Dhul Hijja of the lunar Islamic calendar. It is traditionally marked by the sacrifice of a sheep in remembrance of Allāh's intervention in Abraham's sacrifice of his son Ishmael and the substitution of a sheep. Celebrants partake of the meat and share it with the poor. This sacrifice is not a whole burnt offering or an atonement offering of any kind but rather a thanksgiving and communion offering.

> It is not their meat nor their blood that reaches Allāh: it is your piety that reaches Him . . . (Qur'án 22:37)

> No one should suppose that meat or blood is acceptable to the One True God. It was a pagan fancy that Allāh could be appeased by blood sacrifice. But Allāh does accept the offering of our hearts . . . (Yusuf Alí Commentary)

The Historical Connection of Muhammad with Jewish and Christian Communities

Islam came into existence in sixth century Arabia in response to the idolatry and excesses of the pagan Arabian tribes. Muhammad intended to reintroduce the pure religion of Abraham, which shared a rich heritage with its Jewish and Christian offshoots. According to the Baháʾí understanding, each new revelation is rooted in and subsequently expands upon the teachings of its predecessors. Muhammad was neither Jewish nor Christian. He was raised in Mecca and the presence of Jews or Christians in Mecca is in doubt. Secular scholars have raised questions about the sources of Muhammad's knowledge of them. Nevertheless Muhammad had many opportunities for contacts with both Abrahamic Religions.

Historians mention some 20 Jewish tribes that lived in Arabia during Muhammad's era including two tribes of priests. Those Jews spoke Arabic, were organized into clans like the Arabs, and seem to have fully assimilated the values and customs of desert society. Yemen (Southwestern Arabia) was generally considered a Jewish State until around 523 C.E. and had broad influence on Arabic peoples. Whole tribes had converted to Judaism. Jewish customs and traditions were known and practiced by many Arabs. The Qurʾán describes three tribes of Jews living in Medina when Muhammad fled there in 622 CE.

Despite the fact that Arabia was distant from the Talmudic Centers in Babylon and Palestine, the historical record shows that trade and cultural contacts were extensive. Muʾammed accompanied His uncle on trading missions to Syria, where He had come into contact with Christian monks and with Jewish scholars. Later He was asked to lead a similar expedition Himself on behalf of the wealthy widow Khadijah. Thus it should come as no surprise that the Prophet of Islam would have been exposed to Jewish beliefs and practices, not only the customs of Yemenite and Arabian Jews but the wisdom of the Talmud as well. In this environment, it is most probable that

Muhammad had direct knowledgeable of Jewish practices and His revelation accordingly incorporates a considerable number of them into His religious teachings.

The Qur'án retells various stories of the Old and New Testaments. There are extensive references to Abraham, Moses, David, Jesus and Mary among others. Due to the differences between the Torah and Qur'án in some of the narratives, such as the story of Joseph, some scholars have concluded that cultural contacts were fuzzy, being mediated by time and distance. However, others contend that these differences narrow considerably in light of Talmudic interpretations. One scholar commented "For, astonishingly enough, the Biblical narratives are reproduced in the Qur'án in true Aggadic cloak." (The Haggada or Aggada is a section of the Talmud that specializes in interpreting non-legal matters. See Judaism In Islam, by Abraham Katsh, p. xviii) In other words, the text of the Qur'án does not merely repeat the stories told in the Hebrew Bible, but retells them in the light of the most advanced Judaic Studies of the time. If this viewpoint is correct, it would support the suggestion that Muhammad was familiar with the best of ancient Jewish scholarship.

Similarly, some of the differences between Qur'ánic accounts and the Gospels can be explained by alternate traditions within Christianity. For example, some of the details of the life of Mary found in the Qur'án, but missing from the canonical Gospels, can be traced to the Protoevangelium of James. (See http://www.catholic- forum.com/saints/stj20001.htm)

Islamic Innovations within Sufism

Sufism, or Taßawwuf, grew out of early Islamic asceticism. It was a mystical movement that sought nearness to God through self-denial. While Sufism may have been influenced by the practices of Christian hermits as well as the Neo-Platonism of Alexandria, and the Vedantism of India, it developed into a major movement solidly rooted within the culture of Islam.

The introduction of the element of love, which changed asceticism into mysticism, is ascribed to Rabi'ah al-'Adawiyah (died 801), a woman from Basra who first formulated the Sufi ideal of a love of God that was disinterested, without hope for paradise and without fear of hell. (http://www.franzholzer.de/htmle/esufi2.htm)

The goal of Sufism was a mystical union with the divine. Sexual energy became an analogy for a one-on-one relationship with God. The Song of Songs, a series of love poems found in the Hebrew Bible, may have provided a precedent, Sufism carried the romantic theme to a higher level. Rather than to distain the passions of sexual energy as asceticism did, viewing all passion as an obstacle to union with the divine, Sufism embraced and transformed that energy into a vehicle of union. The devotee was to have no interest in any other aspect of life or any selfish reason for turning to God. The only motivation was the desire of a lover to be with the Beloved. There were no prayers of petition, no requests for favors, no rewards in this life or hereafter. The love of God became an all-consuming passion.

One of Sufism's chief innovations was the focus on prayer as a vehicle for entering the divine presence. Through prayer the worshipper could enter an ecstatic state of nearness to God. Dance and music were used to enhance the experience. Over time, various Christian and Jewish groups adapted Sufi thought and practice to their own devotions. During medieval times, Christian mystic writers such as Saint John of the Cross and Saint Bernard of Clairvaux embellished the theme of the love of God with romantic images. A major theme of the Kabala (dated to around the 11th century) is union with the Shekinah, the feminine aspect of God. The Hasidic Movement arose among the Jews of seventeenth century Poland. Hasidim used music and dance in ways similar to the Sufi dervishes, to achieve spiritual ecstasy.

Other Possible Parallels

Other possible links between Jewish / Christian practice and Muslim practice can be mentioned, although establishing their presence in the time of Muhammad is problematic. Ablutions, prior to prayer, are a marked feature of al-Salat. Jews, likewise make use of water for ritual cleansing. The mikvah is most commonly known as a basin that women use for monthly purification. In earlier ages, it was also a customary method of ritual cleansing for men. Priests in the Jerusalem Temple and Qumran Sect are well known examples. Catholics also use water for ritual purposes prior to prayer and place basins of holy water at the entrance to the Church sanctuary for symbolic cleansing. We do not know what related cleansing rituals may have been used by either Jewish or Christian worshippers in the East from the time of Muhammad , but regardless of whether a direct link existed or not, the principle of purification with water is something shared by all three traditions.

Similarly, with regard to the issue of prayer postures, we have already noted that Jews stand, sit and bow their heads for specific prayers, just as Muslims do for the five-times Salat prayers. Catholics likewise stand, kneel and sit for various part of the Mass. However, we do not know when these practices were instituted or what form they may have taken in 6th century Arabia.

The Catholic rosary is a series of prayers offered daily that begins with an acknowledgment of monotheism in its Trinitarian form, "In the name of the Father, Son and Holy Ghost . . ." This may be seen as a sort of parallel with the opening of al-Salat "In the name of Alláh" (bismilláh).

Islam claims to represent the True Religion of Abraham. Jews and Christians derive their belief and practice from the same roots, as Qur'án freely acknowledges.

> We believe in God, and the revelation given to us, and to
> Abraham, Ismá'íl, Isaac, Jacob, and the Tribes, and that

given to Moses and Jesus, and that given to (all) prophets from their Lord: We make no difference between one and another of them: And we bow to God (in Islám). (Qur'án 2:136)

Recognition of similarities, whether borrowed practices or shared principles, testifies to a shared history. Progressive revelation serves to explain the dynamics of the processes of innovation and preservation of tradition. Daily prayer practices, such as specific hours for prayer, the direction of prayer, etc. had developed over the centuries as a common custom within Judaism and Christianity despite the fact that neither Moses nor Christ had commanded them. In Islam we find the first codification of laws governing daily prayer. The revelation of Muhammad confirmed and expanded upon these customary practices. When viewed in the light, progressive revelation becomes more than updating previous revelation. It becomes an evaluation of the innovations that arose during the preceding Dispensation. The adoption of some of those customs in the subsequent revelation effectively recognizes the value of those initiatives. New spiritual insights are thus seen to be possible, not only during the formative age of each faith, but continuously. While the Manifestations of God (founding prophets) naturally exhibit an extraordinary measure of new light, others, ordinary people who are not inspired prophets, can contribute as well.

Bahá'í Obligatory Prayers

The Bahá'í Age is seen as the age of the world's emerging maturity. Advancement of the individual is stressed. There is no priesthood or clergy. Daily prayer becomes personal and focuses, not on supplication or petition, but upon achieving nearness to God and cultivating spiritual virtues. Congregational ritual is prohibited.

Bahá'u'lláh revealed three obligatory prayers, short, medium and long, in the *Kitáb-i-Aqdas*. Each of these prayers has its own character and associated practices. In previous Dispensations, daily prayer practices such as the prayers to be recited, times of day, positions and so forth developed by custom rather than coming directly from the teachings of the founding prophet. In confirmation of the customary practices of Judaism, Christianity and Islam, Bahá'u'lláh gives specific instructions with each of the obligatory prayers. The worshipper selects one of the three to say each day, at her own option.

Another Bahá'í innovation is the movement of daily prayer from public to private places. The minyan and mass are designed for congregational prayer in synagogue or church. Al-Salat may be public or private but is most widely known by the public call to prayer from the minaret, followed by worshippers dropping whatever they are doing to prostrate themselves in market, street or home. In contrast, Bahá'í obligatory prayer is exclusively private. Congregational use of the three obligatory prayers is prohibited. There are other prayers and other occasions for praying together with others. The purpose of obligatory prayer is to enhance a one-on-one relationship between worshipper and the Divine.

The short prayer is to be said at noon. It is primarily a prayer of praise. Like the Shema and the prayers of the Salat, it proclaims the Oneness of God. "There is none other God but Thee, the Help in Peril, the Self-Subsisting."

The medium prayer is perhaps the most similar to al-Salat. It contains petitions (strengthen my hand O My God) as well as praise (exalted art Thou above my praise) and proclamation of God's uniqueness (I bear witness to Thy unity and oneness.) It is to be said three time a day, requires ablutions, and is accompanied by a series of standing, kneeling and sitting postures.

The writings of Bahá'u'lláh set out specific instruction on ablutions and positions, thus confirming and extending these Islamic innovations which were established by custom rather than prophetic mandate. For example, the instructions accompanying the Medium Prayer state:

To be recited daily, in the morning, at noon and in the evening. Whoso wishes to pray (this one of the three obligatory prayers) let him wash his hands, and while he washeth, let him say: 'Strengthen my hand, O my God, that is may take hold of Thy book . . . ' Let his stand up, facing the Qiblih . . . and say . . . Let him then bend down with hands resting on knees and say . . . (BAHÁ'U'LLÁH, *Kitáb-i-Aqdas*)

The long obligatory prayer is said once a day, at any hour. (Washing in preparation for prayer is specified.) The long prayer is also characterized by various postures.

The long prayer lays emphasis on achieving the mystical experience of entering the presence of God. Incessant prayer, purity of heart, selflessness and detachment are the vehicles that transform the soul and open the door to communion with the divine.

> . . . make of my prayer a fire that will burn away the veils which have shut me out from Thy beauty, and a light that will lead me unto the ocean of Thy Presence.
>
> O Thou in separation from Whom hearts and souls have melted . . . Thou seest, O my Lord, this stranger hastening to his most exalted home beneath the canopy of Thy majesty and within the precincts of Thy mercy . . .
>
> . . . Thy call hath awakened me, and Thy grace hath raised me up and led me unto Thee. Who, otherwise, am I that I should dare to stand at the gate of the city of Thy nearness . . . ?

The intimacy and closeness with the Divine that the long obligatory prayer points to, incorporates the sharing of inner feelings of distress and anguish that we previously saw in David, Jeremiah and Christ.

Thou dost perceive my tears and the sighs I utter and hearest my groanings and my wailings and the lamentations of my heart . . . My trespasses have kept me back from drawing nigh unto Thee . . . and separation from Thee hath destroyed me.

In the long obligatory prayer and elsewhere in the Bahá'í writings, many of the names and attributes given to God exhibit more than the formal relationship of sovereign to subject. God is the Desire of the World, the Beloved of the Nations, the Best Lover and perhaps most simply and powerfully The Friend.

The desire for and achievability of closeness through prayer depicted here is markedly different than the relationship established through animal sacrifices on special occasions at a distant sanctuary. God is now closer in both time and space, and more encompassing as well in the array of emotions that the worshipper shares with God. The desire to draw near to God has been a constant theme of progressive revelation. In ancient Judaism, communion offerings attempted to breach the gap between the worshipper and the Divine by sharing physical food. Procedures for the offerings are set forth in specific detail in the Torah. The choice, fatty pieces of the sacrificial animal were offered upon the altar as God's portion. The people sat within the sacred precincts of the Temple and ate their portion. In Christianity, communion took the form of the bread and wine which stands in the place of blood and flesh in obedience to Christ's direct commandment as recorded in the Gospels. Islam adopted communion sacrifices by custom. But in the Bahá'í Faith, prayer becomes the sole vehicle of communion. There are no communion meals either by mandate or custom. To "enter the presence," to "mourn separation," to "hasten home to the precincts of majesty," to "stand in the Holy City," these are the goals of spiritual communion. The ancient practice of communion had been transformed from physical acts involving food and blood (either literal or symbolic) to a mystical encounter through prayer.

Even the term "commune" has come to signify prayer. The result of achieving a connection to the Divine is "nearness" and "rapture."

> . . . softly recite thou this commune to thy Lord, and say unto Him: O God, my God! Fill up for me the cup of detachment from all things . . . break off from me the shackles of this nether world, draw me with rapture unto Thy supernal realm . . . (ʿABDUʾL–BAHÁ, *Selected Writings of ʿAbduʾl–Bahá*, 174)

> Intone, O my servant, the verses of God . . . and the sweetness of Thy melody will kindle thine own soul. (BAHÁʾUʾLLÁH, *Baháʾí Prayers*, IX)

> Whoso reciteth, in the privacy of his own chambers, the verses revealed by God, the scattering angels of the Almighty will scatter abroad the words uttered by his mouth and cause the heart of every righteous man to throb. (BAHÁʾUʾLLÁH, *Baháʾí Prayers*, IX)

As seen in the third quotation above, Baháʾí detachment does not lead to disengagement from the world. Baháʾuʾlláh forbade monasticism. Detachment represents a freedom to act in the world without becoming entangled or troubled if things do not go as desired.

Further, the Baháʾí definition of prayer is expanded to include loving acts in addition to recited words.

> This is worship: to serve mankind and to minister to the needs of the people. Service is prayer. (ʿABDUʾL–BAHÁ, *Paris Talks*, 176)

The concept of action-prayer, as opposed to verbal prayer, may be the start of a new paradigm. In the past, separation from the world through living on a hilltop or at a monastery has been a way

to focus oneself completely on spiritual things and to avoid the distractions of the world. Now, immersion in the spiritual life can be
attained while living and acting in the world. Service to humanity
when performed in a spirit of reverence becomes in itself a form of
worship. If the service is selfless and wholly for the benefit of others,
a spiritual state of detachment can be achieved that is comparable to
that of the Sufi dervish or the Christian hermit. This form of worship may be called "engaged detachment" as a fusion of mystical and
humanitarian spirituality. This fusion is especially appropriate for
the world's present Age of Emerging Maturity. The foremost spiritual issue facing our planet is the need to let go of self-absorption
and recognize the interconnected oneness of humankind.

Conclusion

Progressive revelation provides a framework for understanding
the interdependence of the world's faiths. It implies the existence of common threads of tradition and practice along with the
emergence of new themes from age to age. The combined affect
of embracing both old and new yields a continuity of belief and
practice on the one hand, and a gradual unfoldment of innovative
teachings on the other.

Chart of Innovations for each Dispensation

Items marked "by written law" were established in the foundational
sacred texts, e.g. Bible, Qur'án. Those marked "by custom" were
established without scriptural mandate. Those marked "sectarian"
were practiced by only a minority of the designated religion.

Pre-Mosaic

- End of human sacrifice (by custom)

• Personal prayer is occasional and petitionary

Jewish

• End of human sacrifice (by written law)

• Sanctuary becomes House of Prayer

• Prayer toward Jerusalem (by custom)

• Synagogue as local house of prayer (by custom)

• Introduction of daily prayer liturgy (by custom)

• Three times daily prayer (by custom)

• Designated body positions used for specific portions of daily prayer service: sitting and standing (by custom)

• Ablutions (sectarian)

• Introduction of praise, thanksgiving and lamentation prayers

Christian

• End of animal sacrifice (by written law)

• Emblematic sacrifice in the form of the Eucharist (by written law)

• Church as local house of prayer (by written law)

• Prayer toward Jerusalem (sectarian and by custom)

• Daily prayer liturgy (by custom)

• Three time daily prayer (sectarian and by custom)

- Designated body positions used for specific portions of daily service (sectarian and by custom)

- Prayer forms include thanksgiving, praise and petitions.

Islam

- Absence of obligatory sacrifice

- Prayer toward Mecca (by written law)

- Five (or three) times daily prayer (by written law)

- Designated body positions used for specific portions of daily prayers (by custom)

- Ablutions (by custom)

- Recitation of specific written prayers (by custom)

- Introduction of nearness prayers (sectarian by custom)

- Prayer forms include thanksgiving, praise and petitions.

Bahá'í

- Prayer toward Bahjí

- Daily obligatory prayers to be recited in private

- Text of prayers specified by written commandment of the founding prophet

- Choice of obligatory prayers

- Ablutions by written law

- Designated body positions by written law

- Forms include thanksgiving, praise, petitions, lamentation and nearness prayers.

From this study, several insights about the nature of progressive revelation emerge. First of all, it is apparent that many of the innovations that are introduced by a given Manifestation of God have precedents during the Dispensation of the previous Manifestation. New spiritual laws, in each age, generally adjust or enhance existing practice.

For example, the practice of praying towards Jerusalem was inaugurated by Solomon, during the Jewish Age, practiced by Jews and Christians thereafter, but not formalized into Law until the time of Muhammad . The direction of prayer (the Qiblih) was later modified by both Muhammad and Bahá'u'lláh, changing it to Mecca and Bahjí respectively. It can be seen therefore that one of the functions of each new revelation is to sort through the innovations of the previous age and to confirm, ban or modify them. The effect is thus more comparable to a course correction that striking out in a totally new direction. We find, for example, the innovation of the synagogue confirmed by Christian law, and the daily prayer practice of Judaism and Christianity confirmed by Islamic Law.

New laws are therefore often the first obligatory implementation of existing practices, rather than brand new innovations. In the context of Bahá'u'lláh's explanation that new revelation is tailored to the needs of the age and limited by the capacity of its recipients, it makes sense that change would be gradual.

We also find innovations from one age that are ignored or explicitly rejected in the next, perhaps due to the lack of any divine sanction in the first place. The Jewish practice of tefillin, the literal wrapping of the head and hands with the words of the Law, was never incorporated in a later revelation. Christian customs of celibate clergy and monastic vows of poverty, were rejected by Muhammad and banned by Bahá'u'lláh. The time between the appearances of the Manifestations of God are often marked by both creativity and sectarian fragmentation of the body of believers. The Prophet, when He appears, examines the innovations of the previous age, confirming some, modifying some, prohibiting others. This serves to distinguish innovations that are beneficial to the spiritual lives of adherents from those that may be harmful, unnecessary or inappropriate to the new age. New revelations clarify the best path for believers, establish a single standard to reconcile old sectarian rivalries and thereby reunite the people.

In the *Kitáb-i-Aqdas*, Bahá'u'lláh taught, "This is the changeless faith of God, eternal in the past, eternal in the future." Thus Bahá'ís would expect to find common threads running through humanity's spiritual history.

Ultimately, in the Bahá'í view, human spiritual history is a single tapestry of interconnected strands.

When seen as a whole the various religions become stages in one comprehensive divine plan. In poetic language, the New Testament describes gentile Christians as branches grafted into the root stock of Judaism. Without Moses and the prophets, Christianity could not exist. The Bahá'í Writings enlarge this analogy, depicting a universal vision of humanity's spiritual development as a single tree with various branches. All are leaves of one tree.

> May fanaticism and religious bigotry be unknown, all humanity enter the bond of brotherhood, souls consort in perfect agreement, the nations of earth at last hoist the banner of truth and the religions of the world enter the divine temple of oneness, for the foundations of the heavenly religions are one reality. ('ABDU'L-BAHÁ, *Foundations of World Unity*, 12, emphasis added)

Appendix A

The Shema (extended version)

Hear, O Israel: The Lord our God is one Lord:
And thou shalt love the Lord thy God with all thine heart,
and with all thy soul, and with all thy might.
And these words, which I command thee this day, shall be
in thine heart:
And thou shalt teach them diligently unto thy children,
and shalt talk of them when thou sittest in thine
house, and when thou walkest by the way, and when
thou liest down, and when thou risest up.
And thou shalt bind them for a sign upon thine hand, and
they shall be as frontlets between thine eyes.
And thou shalt write them upon the posts of thy house,
and on thy gates." (Deuteronomy 6:4-9)
And it shall come to pass, if ye shall hearken diligently
unto my commandments which I command you this
day, to love the Lord your God, and to serve him with
all your heart and with all your soul,
That I will give you the rain of your land in his due
season, the first rain and the latter rain, that thou
mayest gather in thy corn, and thy wine, and thine oil.
And I will send grass in thy fields for thy cattle, that thou
mayest eat and be full.

Take heed to yourselves, that your heart be not deceived,
and ye turn aside, and serve other gods, and worship
them;

And then the Lord's wrath be kindled against you, and he
shut up the heaven, that there be no rain, and that the
land yield not her fruit; and lest ye perish quickly from
off the good land which the Lord giveth you.

Therefore shall ye lay up these my words in your heart
and in your soul, and bind them for a sign upon your
hand, that they may be as frontlets between your eyes.

And ye shall teach them your children, speaking of them
when thou sittest in thine house, and when thou
walkest by the way, when thou liest down, and when
thou risest up.

And thou shalt write them upon the door posts of thine
house, and upon thy gates:

That your days may be multiplied, and the days of your
children, in the land which the Lord swore unto your
fathers to give them, as the days of heaven upon the
earth. (Deuteronomy 11:13-21)

And the Lord spoke unto Moses, saying,

Speak unto the children of Israel, and bid them that they
make them fringes in the borders of their garments
throughout their generations, and that they put upon
the fringe of the borders a ribbon of blue:

And it shall be unto you for a fringe, that ye may look
upon it, and remember all the commandments of the
Lord, and do them; and that ye seek not after your
own heart and your own eyes, after which ye use to go
awhoring:

That ye may remember, and do all my commandments,
and be holy unto your God.

I am the Lord your God, which brought you out of the
land of Egypt, to be your God: I am the Lord your
God. [Numbers 15:37–41)

Introduction to the Amidah (Standing) Prayer Blessed art
Thou, O Lord our God and God of our fathers, God
of Abraham, God of Isaac, and God of Jacob,
The great, might and revered God, the most high God,
Who bestowest loving-kindness and possessest all
things; Who rememberest the pious deeds of the
patriarchs,
And in love will bring a redeemer to their children's
children for thy name's sake.

Appendix B

Modern Orthodox Jewish Prayer Services

The Morning Prayers

- Birchas HaShachar – The morning blessings.

- Pesukei D'Zimra – Verses of Praise from the Psalms.

- Shema and it's Blessings – Shema, preceded and followed by its blessings.

- Amidah – The Eighteen Blessings, which are recited quietly while standing.

- Tachanun – Nefilas Apayim, 'falling on the face'. This prayer is said with head bowed.

- Krias HaTorah – The Reading of the Torah portion.

- Ashrei—Additional Psalms particularly Psalm 20.

- •Aleinu—Concluding prayer.

The Afternoon Prayers

- Ashrei – Ashrei is recited.

- Amidah.

- Tachanun

- •Aleinu

- Ne'ilah – The Closing of the Gates

The Evening Prayers

- Shema and its Blessings

- Amidah

- Aleinu

Appendix C

Text and Instructions for al-Salat

According to Islamic Daily Prayer Manual by Farnaz Khoromi, the words of the daily prayers are composed of the following components, which are combined and repeated in various ways for each of the five prayer times.

- The Intention or Niyyah

- The Call or Takbir

- The Recitation or Qira'ah

- The Bowing or Ruku`

- The Prostration or Sujud

- The Praise or Tasbihat

- The Witnessing or Tashahhud

- The Greeting or Salam

- The Closure or Khatm

  Niyyah: Face the Qiblih (Mecca) and concentrate the heart for the purpose of witnessing God's presence.

  Takbir: Stand. Hold your hands up, thumbs toward your ears, palms out. Say:

Alláho-Akbar God is greater

Qira'ah: Stand and recite the following passages from Qur'án 1:1–7 and 112:1–5:

1.	Besmelláhe rahmane raheem,	In the Name of God, Most Gracious, Most Merciful,
2.	Alhamdo-le-lahe rabbel alameen,	Praise be to God, the Cherisher and Sustainer of the two worlds,
3.	Ar-rahmane raheem,	Most Gracious, Most Merciful
4.	Maleke yomeddeen,	Master of the Day of Religion
5.	Eeyyaka na'bodo	Thee do we worship
6.	Va eeyyaka nasta'een	And Thine aid do we seek,
7.	Eh'dena serat-al- mostagheem,	Show us the straight path
8.	Seratal-lazeena an'amta alayhem	The path of those upon whom Thou hast bestowed Thy Grace,
9.	Ghayr-el-maghzoobe alayhem va la-zaaleen,	Those whose portion is not wrath, and who go not astray.

1.	Besmelláhe rahmane raheem,	In the Name of God, Most Gracious, Most Merciful,
2.	Ghol-ho valla-ho ahad,	Say: He is the unique and only God,
3.	Alláh-ho samad,	Alláh is Omnipresent, (the Eternal, the Absolute),
4.	Lam yaled, va lam yoolad	He begetteth no, Nor is He Begotten,
5.	Va lam yakon lahoo kofavan ahad.	And there is none like unto Him.

Ruku : While standing, lean forward and place hands on knees and say:

Sobhana rabbee-al-zaeeme va be hamde,

Pure is my Creator, the greatest and I praise Him.

Then stand erect and say:

Alláho-Akbar   God is greater

Sujud: (Repeat the following sequence twice.) Prostrate, placing forehead, palms, knees and toes on floor and say:

Sobhana rabbee-al-zaeeme va be hamde,

Pure is my Creator, the greatest and I praise Him.

Then kneel with knees and toes on floor, hands on thighs, back straight and say:

Alláho-Akbar   God is greater

Tasbihat: Stand and repeat the following sequence three times:

1.	Sobhan-alláhe,	Pure is my God,
2.	Val-hamdo-le-lahe,	Praise is for Him,
3.	Va la-elaha ella laho,	There is no God but He,
4.	Valláho-Akbar.	And Alláh is greater.

Tashahhud: Kneel as before and say:

1.	Ashhado an la-elaha-ella laho,		I bear witness that there is no God but Alláh,
2.	Vahdahhoo la sharika lah,		He is the only one and has no partner,
3.	Va ashhado anna Mohammadnan abdohoo		And I bear witness that Muhammad is His servant
4.	Va rassoolah,		and His messenger,
5.	Alláhomma salle ala Mohammaden		O God, bestow thy Light upon Mohammad
6.	Va ale Mohammad.		and His descendent.

Salam: While still kneeling say:

1.	Assalamo alayka ayyoha- nabeeyyo	Greeting to you, O messenger,
2.	Va rahmattolláhe va barakkato,	and the blessings and abundance of God to you.
3.	Assalamo alayna va ala ebadelláhe saleheen,	Greetings to us and the righteous servants of God,
4.	Assalamo alaykom va rahmatolláhe va barakato	Greetings to you all and the blessings and abundance of God.

Khatm: While still kneeling repeat three times:

Alláho-Akbar   God is greater

Bibliography

'Abdu'l-Bahá. *A Traveler's Narrative*. Trans. Edward G. Browne. Wilmette, IL: Bahá'í Publishing Trust, 1988.

— *'Abdu'l-Bahá in London*. London: UK Bahá'í Publishing Trust, 1982.

— *Divine Philosophy*. Comp. Isabel Fraser Chamberlain. Boston, MA: Tudor Press, 1918.

— *Foundations of World Unity*. Comp. Horace, Holley, Wilmette, IL: Bahá'í Publishing Trust, 1968.

— *Memorials of the Faithful*. Trans. Marzieh Gail. Wilmette, IL: Bahá'í Publishing Trust, 1971.

— *Paris Talks*: Addresses Given by 'Abdu'l-Bahá in Paris in 1911–1912. London: Bahá'í Publishing Trust, 1979.

— *The Promulgation of Universal Peace*. Comp. Howard MacNutt. Wilmette, IL: Bahá'í Publishing Trust, 1982.

— *The Secret of Divine Civilization*. Trans. Marzieh Gail and 'Alí-Kula Khan. Wilmette, IL: Bahá'í Publishing Trust, 1990.

— *Selections from the Writings of 'Abdu'l-Bahá*. Comp. Research Department of the Universal House of Justice, trans. Marzieh Gail and a Committee at the Bahá'í World Center. Haifa, Israel: Bahá'í World Center, 1982.

— *Some Answered Questions*. Collected and translated from the Persian by Laura Clifford Barney. Newly Revised by a Committee at the Bahá'í World Centre. Wilmette, IL: Bahá'í Publishing Trust, 2014.

— *Star of the West*. Chicago, IL: 1910–1935.

— *Tablets of 'Abdu'l-Bahá*. Vol. 1–3: Chicago, IL: Bahá'í Publishing Society, 1909.

— *Tablets of the Divine Plan*. Wilmette, IL: Bahá'í Publishing Trust, 1977.

Abel, John. *Apocalypse Secrets: Bahá'í Interpretations of the Book of Revelation*, John Able Books Ltd., 2015.

Angha, Molana Shah Maghsoud Sadegh, *Al-Salat – The Reality of Prayer in Islam*. Washington, D.C.: M.T.O. Shahmaghsoudi Publishing Center, 1998.

Attar, Farid Al-Din, *The Conference of the Birds*, Islámic Poetry

Augustine, St. *The City of God*. Chicago, IL: University of Chicago, Encyclopedia Britannica. Great Books of the Western World, vol. 18, 1952.

The Báb, *Selections from the Writings of the Báb*. Compiled by the Research Department of the Universal House of Justice. Trans. Habib Taherzadeh and a Committee at the Bahá'í World Centre. Haifa, Israel: Bahá'í World Centre, 1982.

Bahá'í Prayers: A Selection of Prayers Revealed by Bahá'u'lláh, the Báb and 'Abdu'l-Bahá. Wilmette, IL: Bahá'í Publishing Trust, 1991.

Bahá'u'lláh, *Epistle to the Son of the Wolf*. Trans. Shoghi Effendi. New edition. Wilmette, IL: Bahá'í Publishing Trust, 1988.

— *Gems of Divine Mysteries*. Haifa, Israel: Bahá'í World Centre, 2002.

— *Gleanings from the Writtings of Bahá'u'lláh*. Trans. Shoghi Effendi. Wilmette, IL: Bahá'í Publishing Trust, 1983.

— *The Hidden Words*, Trans. Shoghi Effendi et al. Wilmette, IL: Bahá'í Publishing Trust, 2002.

— *The Importance of Obligatory Prayer and Fasting*. Trans. and Comp. Research Department of the Universal House of Justice. *The American Bahá'í*, September, 2000.

— *Kitáb-i-Aqdas: The Most Holy Book*. Wilmette, IL: Bahá'í Publishing Trust, 1993.

— *Kitáb-i-Íqán: The Book of Certitude* Trans. Shoghi Effendi. Wilmette, IL: Bahá'í Publishing Trust, 1974.

— *Prayers and Meditations by Bahá'u'lláh* Trans. Shoghi Effendi. Wilmette, IL: Bahá'í Publishing Trust, 1979.

— *The Proclamation of Bahá'u'lláh*. Haifa, Israel: Bahá'í World Centre, 1972.

— *The Seven Valleys and the Four Valleys*. Trans. Marzieh Gail in consultation with 'Alí-Kula Khan. Wilmette, IL: Bahá'í Publishing Trust, 1991

— *The Summons of the Lord of Hosts: Tablets of Bahá'u'lláh*. Trans. Shoghi Effendi et al. Haifa, Israel: Bahá'í World Centre, 2002.

— *Tablets of Bahá'u'lláh revealed after the Kitáb-i-Aqdas*. Comp. Research Department of the Universal House of Justice. Trans. Habib Taherzadeh and a Committee at the Bahá'í World Centre. Haifa, Israel: Bahá'í World Centre, 1978.

Bahiyyih Khanum: The Greatest Holy Leaf. Comp. Research Department at the Bahá'í World Centre. Haifa, Israel: Bahá'í World Centre, 1982.

Barks, Coleman and Green, Michael, *The Illuminated Prayer*. New York, NY: Ballantine Wellspring, 2000.

Bhagavad Gita. Trans. Edwin Arnold. New York, NY: Dover Publications, 1993.

Black Elk. The Sacred Pipe: Black Elk's Account of the Seven Rites of the Oglala Sioux. Recorded and edited by Joseph Epes Brown. Norman, OK: University of Oklahoma Press, 1987.

Catechism of the Catholic Church: Complete and Updated. U.S. Catholic Church, 1995.

Catholic Encyclopedia, http://www.newadvent.org/cathen.html

Compilation of Compilations: By Bahá'u'lláh, Abdu'l-Bahá, Shoghi Effendi, and Universal House of Justice. Comp. Research Department of the Universal House of Justice. Mona Vale: Bahá'í Publications Australia, 1991. Includes compilation on Family Life.

Christian Prayers – The Liturgy of the Hours. New York, NY: Catholic Book Publishing Company, 1976.

Complete ArtScroll Siddur – A New Translation and Anthologized Commentary, Rabbi Nosson Scherman. Brooklyn, NY: Mesorah Publications, Ltd, 1999.

Dhammapada: Sayings of the Buddha. Trans. John Richards, 1993.

The Flower Ornament Scripture: A Translation of the Avatamsaka Sūtra. Trans. Thomas Cleary, 1993.

Gail, Marzieh. *Six Lessons on Islám.* Wilmette, IL: Bahá'í Publishing Trust, 1953.

Heiler, Friedrich, *Prayer – A Study in the History and Psychology of Religion.* Oxford, U.K.: Oxford University Press, 1932.

Holy Bible, King James Version. Grand Rapids: Zondervan Publishing House, 1995.

The Holy Bible, New International Version. Grand Rapids: Zondervan Publishing House, 1984.

Holy Bible: New King James Version. New York, NY: American Bible Society, 1990.

The Holy Scriptures of the Sikhs. Trans. Ernst Trumpp. London: William H. Allen & Co., 1877.

The Holy Qur'án. Trans. Maulana Muhammad Ali. Columbus, OH, Lahore, Inc. USA, 1995.

The Holy Scriptures: Tanakh. Philadelphia, PA: Jewish Publication Society, 1917.

Ibn 'Arabi, Muhyiddin. *Contemplation of the Holy Mysteries and the Rising of Divine Lights.* Trans. Cecilia Twinch and Pablo Beneito. Oxford, UK: Anqa Publishing, 2008.

Idelsohn, Abraham Zebi, *Jewish Liturgy and Its Development.* Toronto, Canada: General Publishing Company, 1995.

Jerusalem Talmud: A Translation and Commentary. Edit. Jacob Neusner. Trans. Tzvee Zahavy et al., 2010.

Katsh, Abraham I., *Judaism in Islam – Biblical and Talmudic Backgrounds of the Koran and its Commentaries.* New York, NY: Sepher-Hermon Press, Inc, 1980.

Khoromi, Farnaz, *Islamic Daily Prayer Manual.* Riverside, CA: M.T.O. Shahmaghsoudi, 1997.

Lights of Guidance: A Bahá'í Reference File. Comp. Helen Hornby. New Delhi, India: Bahá'í Publishing Trust, 1983.

Lights of 'Irfán: Papers Presented at the 'Irfán Colloquia and Seminars, Book Seven. Evanston, IL: Bahá'í National Center, 2006.

Mababharata: Condensed into English Verse. Edit and Trans. Romesh C. Dutt, 1899.

Mishkan T'filah, A Reform Siddur. New York, NY: CCAR Press, 2007.

The Meaning of the Glorious Koran: An Explanatory Translation. Trans. Mohammed Marmaduke Pickthall. Hyderabad-Deccan, India: Government Central Press, 1938.

Pascal, Blaise. *Pensees.* Trans. A. J. Krailsheimer. London, U.K.: Penguin Books Limited, 1995.

The Qur'án. Trans. Abdullah Yusuf Ali. Turkiye: Asir Media, 2015.

Rumi, Jalaluddin. *Mathnawi of Rumi*, Vol. 1–6. Trans. E. H. Whinfield, 1899.

St. Francis of Asissi. *Prayer of St. Francis.*

St. John of the Cross. *Ascent of Mount Carmel.* New York, NY: Magisterium Press, 2015.

Shoghi Effendi, *The Advent of Divine Justice.* Wilmette, IL: Bahá'í Publishing Trust, 1984.

— *Citadel of Faith: Messages to America, 1947–1957.* Wilmette, IL: Bahá'í Publishing Trust, 1965.

— *Directives from the Guardian.* New Delhi, India: Bahá'í Publishing Trust, 1973.

— *God Passes By.* Wilmette, IL: Bahá'í Publishing Trust, 1974.

— *The World Order of Bahá'u'lláh.* Wilmette, IL: Bahá'í Publishing Trust, 1991.

— *The Unfolding Destiny of the British Bahá'í Community: The Messages of the Guardian of the Bahá'í Faith to the Bahá'ís of the British Isles.* London, U.K.: Bahá'í Publishing Trust, 1981.

Srimad Bhāgavatam of Sri Krishnadvaipāyana Vyāsa. Madras, India: Sree Gaudiya Math, 1986.

Swami Kriyananda. *Awaken to Superconsciousness: How to Use Meditation for Inner Peace, Intuitive Guidance, and Greater Awareness.* Nevada City, CA: Crystal Clarity Publishers, 2008.

Tanakh: The Holy Scriptures – The New JPS Translation. Philadelphia, PA: The Jewish Publication Society, 1985.

Tao Te Ching: Lao Tzu's Book of the Way and of Righteousness. Trans. Charles Johnson. Kstetra Books, 2014.

The Translation of the Meanings of Sahih Al Bukhari Arabic English. Vol. 1–9. Trans. Muhammad Muhsin Khan. Egypt: Al Saadawi Publications, 1959.

The Upanishads. Trans. Eknath Easwaran. Tomalas, CA: Nilgiri Press, 2007.

Weiss, Zeev. "The Sepphoris Synagogue Mosaic," *Biblical Archeology Review*, September / October, 2000.

Zend-Avesta. Trans. Trans. James Darmesteter. New York, NY: The Christian Literature Company,1898.

www.ingramcontent.com/pod-product-compliance
Lightning Source LLC
Chambersburg PA
CBHW080527090426

42733CB00015B/2511